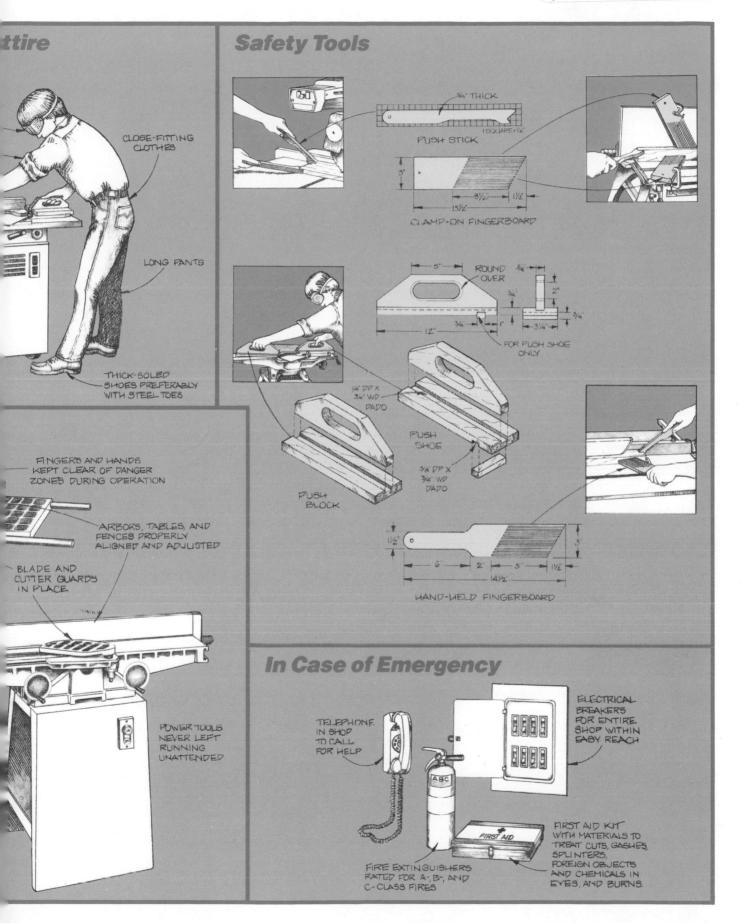

ttire

CLOSE-FITTING CLOTHES

LONG PANTS

THICK-SOLED SHOES PREFERABLY WITH STEEL TOES

FINGERS AND HANDS KEPT CLEAR OF DANGER ZONES DURING OPERATION

ARBORS, TABLES, AND FENCES PROPERLY ALIGNED AND ADJUSTED

BLADE AND CUTTER GUARDS IN PLACE

POWER TOOLS NEVER LEFT RUNNING UNATTENDED

Safety Tools

¾" THICK

1 SQUARE = ½"

PUSH STICK

3"

8½"   1½"

13½"

CLAMP-ON FINGERBOARD

5"   ROUND OVER   ¾"

¾"   2"

¾"

12"   ¾" 1"   3¼"   ¾"

FOR PUSH SHOE ONLY

¼" DP X ¾" WD DADO

PUSH SHOE

PUSH BLOCK

⅜" DP X ¾" WD DADO

1½"   3"

6"   2"   5"   1½"

14½"

HAND-HELD FINGERBOARD

In Case of Emergency

TELEPHONE IN SHOP TO CALL FOR HELP

ELECTRICAL BREAKERS FOR ENTIRE SHOP WITHIN EASY REACH

ABC

FIRST AID

FIRST AID KIT WITH MATERIALS TO TREAT CUTS, GASHES, SPLINTERS, FOREIGN OBJECTS AND CHEMICALS IN EYES, AND BURNS.

FIRE EXTINGUISHERS RATED FOR A-, B-, AND C-CLASS FIRES

·BUILD·IT·BETTER·YOURSELF·
WOODWORKING PROJECTS

Workshop Tables, Cabinets, and Jigs

Collected and Written
by Nick Engler

Rodale Press
Emmaus, Pennsylvania

Printed in the United States of America on acid-free ∞, recycled paper ♻

If you have any questions or comments concerning this book, please write:

Rodale Press
Book Reader Service
33 East Minor Street
Emmaus, PA 18098

Series Editor: Jeff Day
Managing Editor/Author: Nick Engler
Editor: Roger Yepsen
Copy Editor: Mary Green
Graphic Designer: Linda Watts
Graphic Artists: Mary Jane Favorite
                 Chris Walendzak
Photography: Karen Callahan
Cover Photography: Mitch Mandel
Cover Photograph Stylist: Janet C. Vera
Proofreader: Hue Park
Typesetting by Computer Typography, Huber Heights, Ohio
Interior Illustrations by O'Neil & Associates, Dayton, Ohio
Endpaper Illustrations by Mary Jane Favorite
Produced by Bookworks, Inc., West Milton, Ohio

Library of Congress Cataloging-in-Publication Data

Engler, Nick.
    Workshop tables, cabinets, and jigs / collected and written
  by Nick Engler : [photography by Karen Callahan].
        p.   cm.—(Build-it-better-yourself woodworking
      projects)
    ISBN 0–87857–939–7 hardcover
    ISBN 0–87857–940–0 paperback
    1. Workshops—Equipment and supplies—Design and
  construction. 2. Woodwork—Equipment and supplies—
  Design and construction. I. Title.   II. Series: Engler, Nick.
  Build-it-better-yourself woodworking projects.
  TT152.E54   1990
  684'.08'028—dc20   90–8833
                                                                 CIP

Distributed in the book trade by St. Martin's Press

    4 6 8 10 9 7 5 3   hardcover
  2 4 6 8 10 9 7 5 3 1   paperback

Contents

Creating a Workable Workshop

There isn't a woodworker on earth who, at one time or another, hasn't wished for a bigger workshop and more tools. However, it isn't the amount of space or the number of tools that make a pleasant, productive workshop — it's how well you *plan* the shop. A thoughtful design helps create a good working atmosphere. The work flows smoothly; there are fewer hassles. You feel comfortable in your workshop; it works for you. So you spend more time there — and accomplish more. The arrangement of the tools, the placement of the workbench, the availability of storage — in short, the overall design of the workshop — contribute more to getting the job done than the amount of space or the number of tools.

The point is: It's not what you have, but how well you use it. And *planning* is the first step to using your shop and the tools in it to the greatest advantage. Design your workshop — don't just let it happen. If it has already happened and your shop is not working out as well as you'd like, here are some tips to help it function better.

Working with What You Have

There is no one way to put together a good workshop; each shop must be custom-tailored to the woodworker. However, some commonsense rules may help: (1) Keep it simple. (2) Make small improvements as you go. (3) Think about each tool carefully — how you're going to use it and where you're going to keep it — before you add it to your shop. And above all, (4) don't rush things. Putting together a shop is like any other woodworking project. If you hurry it along or try to do too many things at once, you make mistakes. Great shops — like great woodworkers — evolve slowly, over time.

So what's the first step in setting up a new workshop or changing something about your present one? Try not to do anything until you've asked yourself a few questions: What sort of space is available? What sort of woodworking do you want to do? What sorts of tools and materials do you like to work with?

Space — If you're setting up a new shop, your first inclination may be to place it wherever you have the most room. But the amount of space shouldn't be your only concern. Is the space heated, or can you easily add heat so you'll be able to work all year round? Is the space too damp to safely store tools and lumber? Will sawdust clog nearby furnace filters or interfere with the laundry and other utilities? Is the area safe from children and thieves? Consider *all* the factors.

If you've already set up a shop, then the question isn't where to put it, but how much free space is available. If you're like most woodworkers, there's probably not a lot. A little rearranging can usually create more space, but consider whether the new arrangement will enhance the work flow or create a bottleneck. Although you can always find a way to shoehorn a new tool into your shop, it may interfere with the tools you already have. On the other hand, it's possible that the advantages of the new tool outweigh the inconvenience of a little crowding. Once again, consider all the factors.

Work interests — Under the general heading of "woodworking," there are dozens of specialties, each of which requires a different set of tools. Chances are you're interested in more than one of them. Before you buy all the tools you think you need, remember the first rule: Keep it simple.

If you're a novice, equip your shop to do the first project on your list, and *nothing* else. You learn a great deal during the course of a single major project, and that can significantly affect your woodworking ambitions. Make the necessary changes and additions to your shop so you can go on to the next project, but try to keep these changes small.

As you get a few woodworking projects under your belt, the changes and additions will be fewer and further between. But you still need to carefully consider each new acquisition, especially as your shop becomes more crowded.

Tools and materials — There are several ways to accomplish every woodworking operation using different tools and materials. But as you spend more time in your shop, you'll find there are specific tools and materials that you prefer. Pay close attention to these preferences as they develop. When you build or modify a workshop, follow them. Woodworking is a highly personal activity, and workshops are a personal space. Yours should fit like an old shoe.

On the other hand, don't be afraid to try new tools or materials. This is what keeps woodworking interesting and makes your workshop an exciting place. But build on what you already know. Radical changes are sometimes disastrous, not because the tools and materials are inferior to what you've been using but because you don't yet have the experience to use them effectively.

Work Flow

Once you've determined where you're going to put your shop (or that you will rearrange your present shop), think about where you'll put everything in it.

The arrangement of tools, workbench, and other items will determine, more than any other factor, just how workable your workshop is for you. It creates a particular *work flow*. The work progresses from tool to tool — or area to area — as projects are built. As long as this flow is smooth and logical, the work moves quickly and comfortably.

How do you create a good work flow? First of all, consider how you move about the shop. Most woodworkers move among three general areas — workbench, stationary power tools, and storage cabinets or pegboards where they keep hand tools and materials. Arrange your workshop to create a *work triangle* between these three areas, with an open space between the corners of the triangle. This open triangle allows you to move from one area to the next quickly and easily, without having to walk through one area to get to another.

How do you set up or enhance a work triangle? To a large extent, that depends on the shape of your workshop. Here are suggestions for dealing with four common shapes:

Rectangular — Most of the available shop space around your home is rectangular — the garage, the basement, an outbuilding, or a spare room. This is fortunate, since a rectangular shop can be the easiest to set up and the most comfortable to work in. To set up a shop, simply put the workbench near one wall, storage against another, and the power tools against the remaining two walls. Presto! A work triangle. (See Figure 1.) There are no obstructions, except perhaps architectural features such as doors, windows, or stairs.

Obstructed — Shop areas frequently have obstructions, such as support posts, furnaces, or water heaters. As long as these are near walls, they are little bother. But when they take up space near the middle of the floor, they can interrupt the work flow.

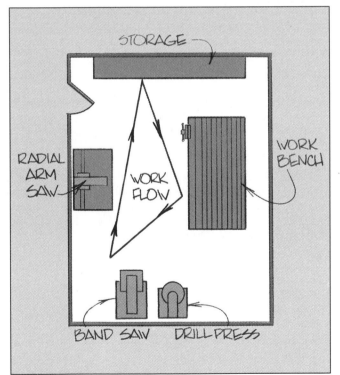

1/When working with a **rectangle,** set up the shop with a clear area in the middle of the tools, workbench, and storage.

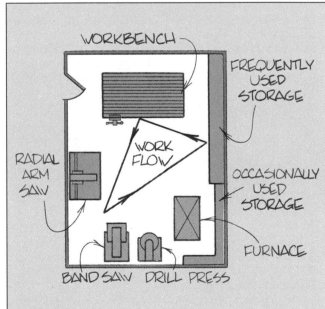

2/If your shop space is **obstructed** by posts or utilities, use the area behind the obstruction to store occasionally used tools and materials.

To set up a shop in an obstructed area, first decide where there is the most clear space. Place the workbench and power tools here. Then divide the storage into two parts — tools and materials that are used *frequently* and those used *occasionally*. Store the frequently used items in front or to one side of the obstruction, and the occasionally used items behind it. (See Figure 2.)

L-shaped — L-shaped areas are particularly common in buildings that have been enlarged over the years. The L-shape is one of the hardest to use comfortably. If you put storage in one arm of the L and power tools in the other, with the workbench at the juncture, then you will be constantly walking through the workbench area and dancing around partially completed projects. There is no real work triangle, and the work flow is impeded. The only solution to this dilemma is to treat the juncture of the L like an obstruction. Decide which of the arms has the most floor space, and place the workbench and power tools in that area. Put frequently used materials in the smaller arm of the L, as near as possible to the juncture. Put the things that you don't need as often further back, at the tip of the small arm. (See Figure 3.)

Long and narrow — What if the walls of your workshop are so close together that you can't place a workbench and power tools against opposing walls and still have space to walk in between? What if the best available space is long and narrow? If this is the case, set up a "galley" shop. Place the workbench, tools, and storage all against one long wall, so you can walk the length of the shop without having to step around anything. Position the workbench between the power tools and the storage. Since the workbench is where most woodworkers spend most of their time, this arrangement will allow easy access to the other areas. (See Figure 4.)

Safety and Comfort

In addition to careful planning and arranging, you must also set up a shop for safety and comfort. With each new addition or improvement, work toward creating a hassle-free environment that promotes good shop practice. This helps to prevent not only major disasters but also minor inconveniences such as stumbling over power cords or straining your eyes to see a mark on a board. These annoyances can leave you tired, irritable, and stressed-out from working in your own shop — the

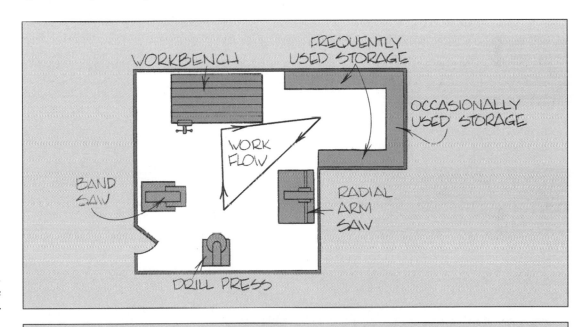

3/In an **L-shaped** workshop, use the smallest arm for storage, with occasionally used items closest to the back.

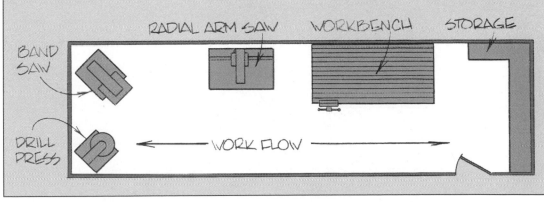

4/In a **long and narrow** workshop, always place the workbench between the storage and the power tools.

place you built as a refuge from all the other things in your life that make you tired, irritable, and stressed-out.

Safety and comfort, like craftsmanship, come from close attention to details. Here's a brief checklist of things to consider:

■ *Safety tools and jigs* — Keep them where you need them. Place safety glasses, ear protectors, and a dust mask in a central location. Store pushsticks and push blocks near the tools with which they're used.

■ *Traffic* — Arrange your workbench and tools so you have clear, straight walkways in your shop.

■ *Electrical power* — Make sure you have plenty of outlets on every wall so you don't need to run power cords across the floor. Also make sure there is enough power. Most home workshop power tools require 20-amp circuits with 12-gauge wire.

■ *Lighting* — Bad lighting is not only unsafe, it's depressing. Install adequate lighting and place it so you won't cast a shadow on your work, no matter where you stand.

■ *Ventilation* — If needed, install a ventilating fan to keep dust and fumes from accumulating in the workshop air. This does more than clear the air — it prevents moisture from condensing on your tools and corroding them.

■ *Sawdust control* — Keep a powerful vacuum in your shop, capable of moving at least 160 cubic feet of air per minute (CFM) and generating 80″ of static pressure (SP) — look for the ratings on the label. Whenever you can, hook this vacuum to your tools as you work.

■ *Emergencies* — Be prepared. Every shop should have a *fire extinguisher* (rated ABC, for ordinary, elec-

trical, and chemical fires), a *first-aid kit* with the items necessary to treat major and minor cuts, burns, splinters, and foreign objects or chemicals in the eye, and a *telephone* to call for help if you need it.

■ *Custom tailoring* — Workbenches, shelves, and tools should all be at a comfortable height. Pay no attention to lists of "standard" heights; tailor the furniture and fittings in your shop to you.

■ *Noise reduction* — Line the walls and ceiling of your shop with something soft, such as fiberboard or "builder's board," to absorb the din of the power tools.

■ *Heating and cooling* — Filter the shop air before it's pumped through your furnace or air conditioner, and clean or change these filters frequently.

■ *Aesthetics* — Build shop furniture and fittings with the same care that you'd take when doing any other woodworking project. Make them look nice — you'll be a lot happier in a shop filled with examples of your excellent craftsmanship.

A Parting Thought

Setting up a workable workshop is a perpetual process — it's a project that you'll never finish. Each time you build something new in your workshop, you'll add to your woodworking knowledge. You'll think of new tools that you might need and new ways to arrange your shop to make it safer, more efficient, or more comfortable. Because your growth as a craftsman never ends, the best of all possible workshops will always be one new tool, one better workbench, or one new storage cabinet away.

Creating a Personal Shop

Your workshop should fit you like a comfortable pair of old shoes. When building workbenches, cabinets, and tool stands, you don't have to build them to traditional dimensions. *Customize* them to fit *you!* Measure your own maximum reach mid-chest, waist, and mid-thigh, then use these measurements to determine the height of the various fixtures in the shop. Refer to the drawing for suggestions on where to place specific tools and work surfaces.

Router Cabinet

The router is unusual in that you can use it as either a portable tool or a stationary power tool. In its normal configuration, you hold it in your hands and move it across the work. With a special table or cabinet to hold the router, you move the work across the tool. To take full advantage of the router's potential, you must be able to do both. For this reason, a table or cabinet is an important router accessory.

The router cabinet shown has several special features. While most cabinets are designed to hold small routers with 6"-diameter bases, this one will accommodate a more powerful 7" router as well. The area under its worktable has enough vertical clearance to allow the use of a plunge router. This space also lets you quickly adjust the height of the router bit above the table.

Finally, this cabinet offers storage space. There are two drawers for bits, collars, and guides. Beneath these, an enclosed cupboard holds jigs, templates, and larger router accessories.

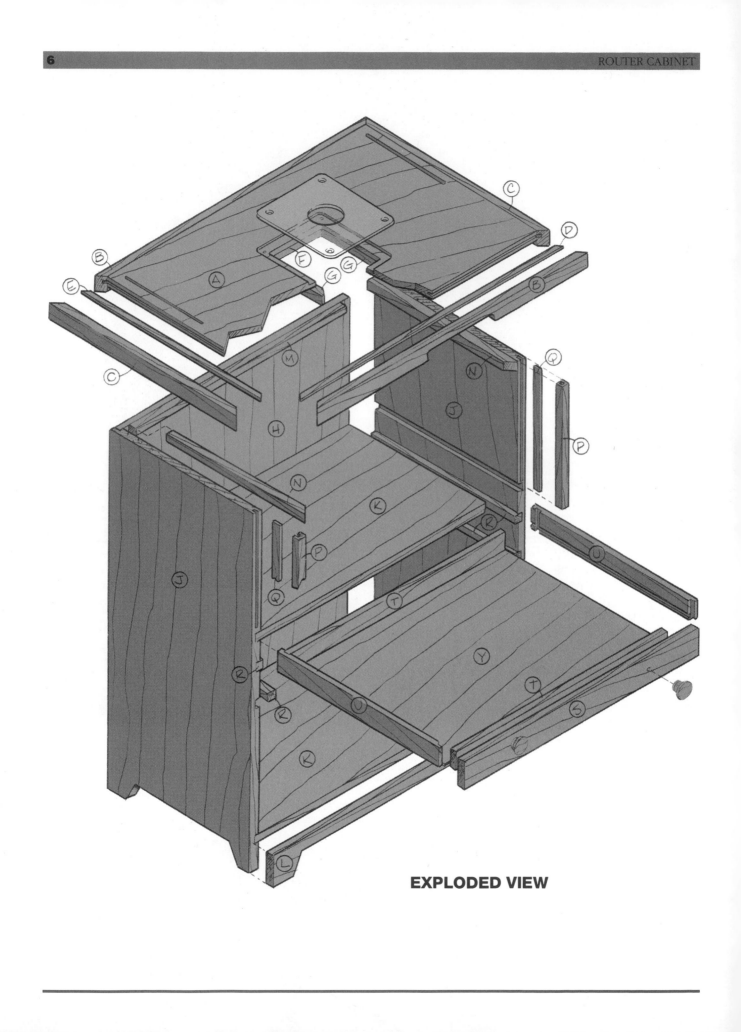

EXPLODED VIEW

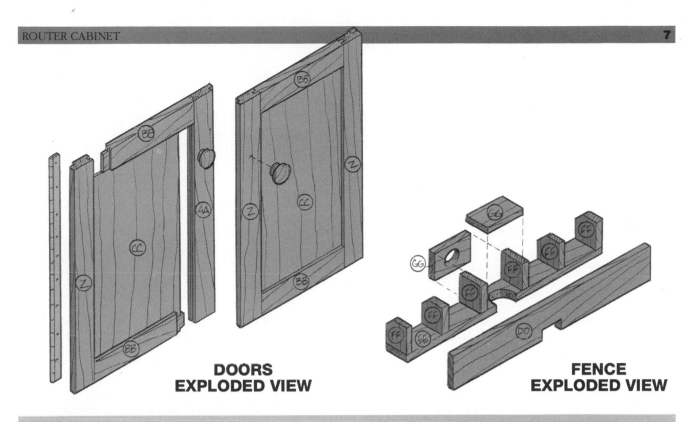

**DOORS
EXPLODED VIEW**

**FENCE
EXPLODED VIEW**

Materials List

FINISHED DIMENSIONS

PARTS

A. Worktable* $^{3}/_{4}$" x 19 $^{1}/_{4}$" x 28 $^{1}/_{2}$"

B. Front/back
trim** (2) $^{3}/_{4}$" x 1 $^{1}/_{2}$" x 30"

C. Side trim** (2) $^{3}/_{4}$" x 1 $^{1}/_{2}$" x 20 $^{3}/_{4}$"

D. Front/back
splines*** (2) $^{1}/_{4}$" x $^{3}/_{4}$" x 29 $^{1}/_{4}$"

E. Side splines*** (2) $^{1}/_{4}$" x $^{3}/_{4}$" x 20"

F. Back short
cleat** $^{3}/_{4}$" x $^{3}/_{4}$" x 7 $^{1}/_{2}$"

G. Side short
cleats** (2) $^{3}/_{4}$" x $^{3}/_{4}$" x 9"

H. Back*** $^{3}/_{4}$" x 25 $^{1}/_{4}$" x 35 $^{1}/_{4}$"

J. Sides*** (2) $^{3}/_{4}$" x 16" x 35 $^{1}/_{4}$"

K. Shelves*** (2) $^{3}/_{4}$" x 15 $^{5}/_{8}$" x 25 $^{1}/_{4}$"

L. Toeboard** $^{3}/_{4}$" x 3" x 26"

M. Long back cleat** $^{3}/_{4}$" x $^{3}/_{4}$" x 23"

N. Long side
cleats** (2) $^{3}/_{4}$" x $^{3}/_{4}$" x 15 $^{1}/_{4}$"

P. Facing** (2) $^{3}/_{4}$" x $^{3}/_{4}$" x 12 $^{3}/_{4}$"

Q. Facing
splines*** (2) $^{1}/_{4}$" x $^{3}/_{4}$" x 12 $^{3}/_{4}$"

R. Drawer
supports** (4) $^{3}/_{4}$" x $^{3}/_{4}$" x 15 $^{1}/_{4}$"

S. Drawer
faces** (2) $^{3}/_{4}$" x 3 $^{7}/_{16}$" x 26"

T. Top drawer front/
back** (2) $^{1}/_{2}$" x 1 $^{15}/_{16}$" x 23 $^{15}/_{16}$"

U. Top drawer
sides** (2) $^{1}/_{2}$" x 1 $^{15}/_{16}$" x 15 $^{1}/_{4}$"

V. Bottom drawer front/
back** (2) $^{1}/_{2}$" x 2 $^{11}/_{16}$" x 23 $^{15}/_{16}$"

W. Bottom drawer
sides** (2) $^{1}/_{2}$" x 2 $^{11}/_{16}$" x 15 $^{1}/_{4}$"

Y. Drawer bottoms***
(2) $^{1}/_{4}$" x 14 $^{3}/_{16}$" x 23 $^{7}/_{8}$"

Z. Door stiles** (3) $^{3}/_{4}$" x 2" x 12 $^{7}/_{10}$"

AA. Inside left
door stile** $^{3}/_{4}$" x 2 $^{5}/_{16}$" x 12 $^{7}/_{10}$"

BB. Door rails** (4) $^{3}/_{4}$" x 2" x 11"

CC. Door
panels*** (2) $^{1}/_{4}$" x 9 $^{1}/_{8}$" x 9 $^{11}/_{16}$"

DD. Fence*** $^{3}/_{4}$" x 4 $^{1}/_{2}$" x 30"

EE. Fence base*** $^{3}/_{4}$" x 3" x 30"

FF. Fence
braces*** (6) $^{3}/_{4}$" x 3" x 3 $^{3}/_{4}$"

GG. Dust collector
top/back*** (2) $^{3}/_{4}$" x 3" x 5 $^{1}/_{2}$"

*Make from laminate-covered
particleboard.
**Make from solid stock.
***Make from cabinet-grade plywood.

HARDWARE

$^{3}/_{8}$" x 8 $^{1}/_{2}$" x 8 $^{1}/_{2}$" Acrylic plastic

#8 x 1 $^{1}/_{4}$" Flathead wood screws
(48–60)

4d Finishing nails (16)

$^{5}/_{16}$" x 2" Carriage bolts (2)

$^{5}/_{16}$" Wing nuts (2)

$^{5}/_{16}$" Flat washers (2)

1 $^{1}/_{2}$" x 12 $^{3}/_{16}$" Piano hinges and
mounting screws (2)

1 $^{1}/_{2}$" Drawer/door pulls (6)

Door catch

Combination switch/outlet

Metal switch box and outlet plate

Cable/box connector

14/3 Electrical appliance cord (10')

Grounded plug

1 Select the stock and cut it to size.

To build this project, you'll need approximately 10 board feet of hardwood, one 4' x 8' sheet of ¾" cabinet-grade plywood, a 4' x 4' sheet of ¼" cabinet-grade plywood, and a 2' x 4' sheet of ¾" particleboard. Select a very hard wood, such as birch, maple, or oak, and plywood with a matching veneer. The cabinet shown was made from birch and birch-veneer plywood.

The particleboard must be covered on one side with a plastic laminate. To save time and money, look for a large "sink cutout" left over from a countertop. These are available at most building supply houses, though they aren't always in stock. If you can't find one, ask a local cabinetmaker to save you the cutout the next time he installs a kitchen cabinet with a double sink.

After gathering the materials, cut them all to the sizes shown in the Materials List, except for the trim, the drawer parts, and the door parts. Cut the trim about 1" longer than specified. Make the drawer and door parts later, after you assemble the case.

2 Make the cutout in the worktable.

The router mounts to an acrylic plastic base which, in turn, mounts in a cutout in the middle of the worktable. Make this cutout with a router and a saber saw.

To make the cutout, first clamp four scraps of wood to the worktable stock to form a square — these scraps will guide the router. The dimensions of this square are determined by the diameter of the router base. You want to rout a groove around a square that has *outside* dimensions of 8½" x 8½". To calculate the *inside* dimensions of the scrap wood square, add the groove dimensions to the diameter of the router base, and subtract the diameter of the bit. For instance, if you use a ¾"-diameter bit to cut this groove, and your router base is 7" across, the inside dimensions of the scrap wood square should be 14¾" x 14¾" (or, 8½" plus 7 minus ¾" equals 14¾").

Mount a ¾"-diameter bit in the router and cut a ¾"-wide, ⅜"-deep groove around the square centered in the worktable stock. (See Figure 1.) Mark the bottom of the groove and make the cutout with a saber saw. (See Figure 2.) When you've finished, the cutout should be 7½" square, with a ½"-wide, ⅜"-deep rabbet all around it.

Note: You also could make the cutout first, *then* rout the rabbet. But if you follow the procedure given here, the router will be easier to control because its entire base is supported as you cut the groove.

1/Before you make the cutout for the router plate, rout a square groove in the center of the worktable. Clamp scraps to the table to guide the router, and keep the router base pressed against these scraps as you cut. Make the groove in several passes, cutting just ¹⁄₁₆"–⅛" deeper with each pass.

2/Mark the bottom of the groove where you want to make the cutout. Drill ½"-diameter holes through the waste to start the cuts, then make the cutout with a saber saw. Work slowly to avoid chipping the particleboard.

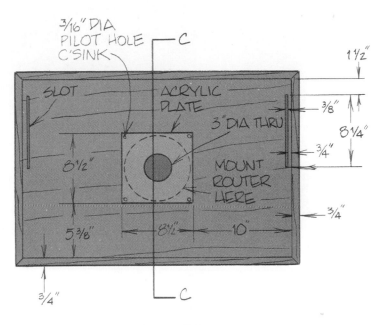

TOP VIEW

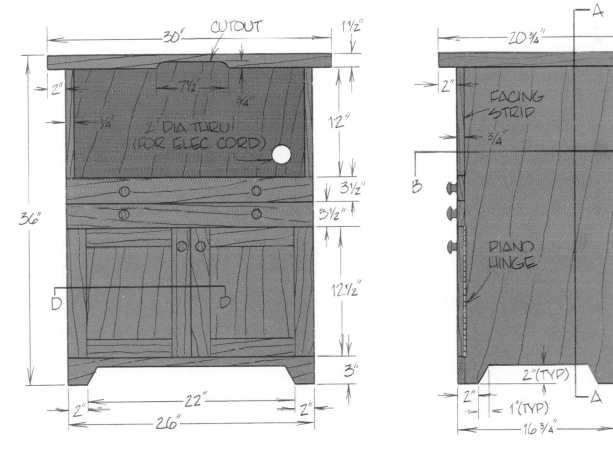

FRONT VIEW **SIDE VIEW**

3 Cut the slots in the worktable.

3 **Cut the slots in the worktable.** The fence bolts to the worktable and travels back and forth in two long slots on either side of the worktable. Cut these slots with a router.

Clamp a scrap of wood to the worktable to guide the router. Once again, the position of this scrap is determined by the diameter of the router base. Clamp another scrap beneath the table — this will keep the particleboard from chipping when the router bit breaks through. Mount a ³/₈″-diameter bit in the router and cut two ³/₈″-wide, 9″-long slots in the worktable, one near each side, as shown in the *Top View*. (See Figure 3.)

3/Rout the mounting slots for the fence, using a scrap to guide the router. Make each slot in several passes, routing just ¹/₁₆″–¹/₈″ deeper with each pass. Take very shallow cuts when routing particleboard; it's more brittle than wood.

4 Cut the spline grooves for the trim and facing.

4 **Cut the spline grooves for the trim and facing.** Both the trim and the facing are attached to the cabinet assembly with plywood splines. Cut ¹/₄″-wide, ³/₈″-deep grooves for these splines with either a router and a straight bit or a dado cutter. Cut the grooves in the *edges* of the worktable and sides, and the *faces* of the trim and facing. (See Figures 4 and 5.) Note that the grooves in the sides are *blind* — stop these cuts when the grooves are 12³/₄″ long.

Square the blind ends of the grooves in the sides with a mortising chisel.

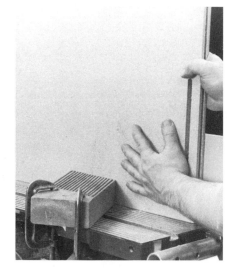

*4/Cut spline grooves in the edge of the worktable and the sides. If you use a dado cutter, keep the **top** face of the worktable and the **outside** face of the sides against the fence.*

*5/Cut the spline grooves in the trim and facing with the same setup. Keep the **top** edge of the trim and the **outside** edge of the facing against the fence as you cut.*

5 Attach the short cleats and the trim to the worktable.

5 **Attach the short cleats and the trim to the worktable.** Cut the shape of the front trim, as shown in the *Front View*. (This cutout enables you to see and reach the shaft of the router easily.) Finish sand the outside face of the trim parts. Miter the ends at 45°, fitting around the perimeter of the worktable. Glue them in place with splines.

Round the front ends of the side cleats, so you won't scrape your hands when changing router bits. Glue the cleats to the bottom face of the worktable, making their inside edges flush with the edges of the worktable cutout.

6 Cut the joinery in the sides and back.

The parts of the case are joined with simple dadoes and rabbets. Using a router or a dado cutter, cut ³/₄"-wide, ³/₈"-deep dadoes in the sides and back to hold the shelves and drawer supports. Also cut ³/₄"-wide, ³/₈"-deep rabbets in the back edge of the sides to hold the back. The positions of these joints are shown in *Section A* and *Section C*.

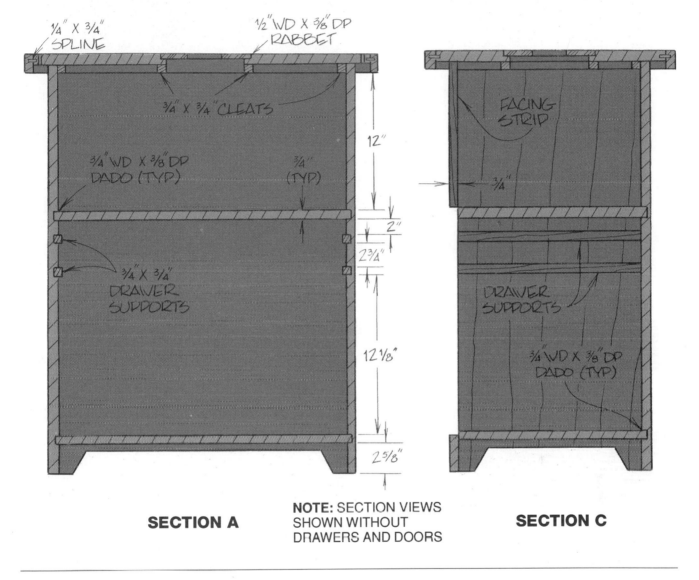

SECTION A

NOTE: SECTION VIEWS SHOWN WITHOUT DRAWERS AND DOORS

SECTION C

7 Cut the shapes of the toeboard, sides, and back.

Lay out the shapes of the feet at the bottom edges of the toeboard, sides, and back, as shown in the *Front View* and *Side View*. Cut these shapes with a saber saw or band saw, then sand the sawed edges.

8 Drill the electrical access hole in the back.

Using a hole saw or a multispur bit, make a 2"-diameter hole in the back for the electrical cord. The placement of this hole is not critical, but it must be *above* the dado for the top shelf.

9 Assemble the case.

Assemble the case. Glue the drawer supports in the sides, then assemble the sides, back, and shelves with glue and screws. Finish sand the toeboard, and attach it to the case assembly with glue and screws. Counterbore and countersink each of the screws, then cover the heads with wooden plugs. Sand the plugs and the joints clean and flush.

Miter the front ends of the long side cleats. Drill and countersink pilot holes in these cleats through both the edges *and* the faces, as shown in the *Worktable Joinery Detail* and *Section B.* The positions of these pilot holes are not critical, but they should be evenly spaced every

6"–8". Stagger them so the holes in the edges don't go through the holes in the faces.

Attach the facing to the front edges of the sides with glue and splines. The top ends of this facing should be flush with the top edges of the sides.

Use glue and screws to attach the long cleats to the inside faces of the sides and back. The top edges of the cleats should be flush with the top edges of the sides and back.

Use screws (but do *not* glue) to attach the worktable assembly to the case. This will allow you to remove the worktable should you need to replace or repair it.

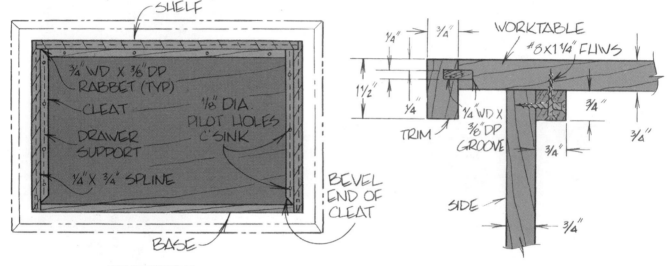

SECTION B

NOTE: SECTION VIEW
SHOWN WITHOUT
DRAWERS AND DOORS

WORKTABLE JOINERY DETAIL

10 Cut the drawer parts.

Cut the drawer parts. Measure the dimensions of the assembled case. If the measurements have changed from those shown in the drawings, make the necessary changes in the dimensions of the drawer parts. Cut the drawer parts to size.

TRY THIS! Many craftsmen prefer to build drawers about 1/16" oversize, then plane and sand them to a perfect fit.

11 Cut the drawer joinery.

Cut the drawer joinery. Like the case, the drawers are assembled with simple rabbets, dadoes, and grooves. Cut the following joints:

- 1/2"-wide, 1/4"-deep rabbets in the front ends of the sides, as shown in the *Drawer/Top View,* to attach the fronts

- 1/2"-wide, 1/4"-deep dadoes near the back ends of the sides, to hold the backs
- 1/4"-wide, 1/4"-deep grooves in the fronts, backs, and sides to hold the bottoms

12

Assemble and fit the drawers. Finish sand the drawer faces. Glue the drawer fronts, backs, and sides together, reinforcing the rabbet and dado joints with finishing nails. Set the heads of the nails slightly below the surface of the wood. As you assemble the drawers, slide the bottoms in place but do *not* glue them. Let them float in their grooves. Glue the drawer faces in place and attach drawer pulls.

Sand all joints clean and flush, then insert the drawers in the case. Test the sliding action. If they bind, plane or sand a little stock from the drawer sides until the drawer moves in and out smoothly.

13

Cut the door parts. With the drawers in place, measure the dimensions of the door opening in the case. If the measurements have changed from those shown in the drawings, make the necessary changes in the dimensions of the door parts. Cut the door parts to size.

TRY THIS! As with drawers, many craftsmen prefer to build doors slightly oversize, then plane and sand them to fit.

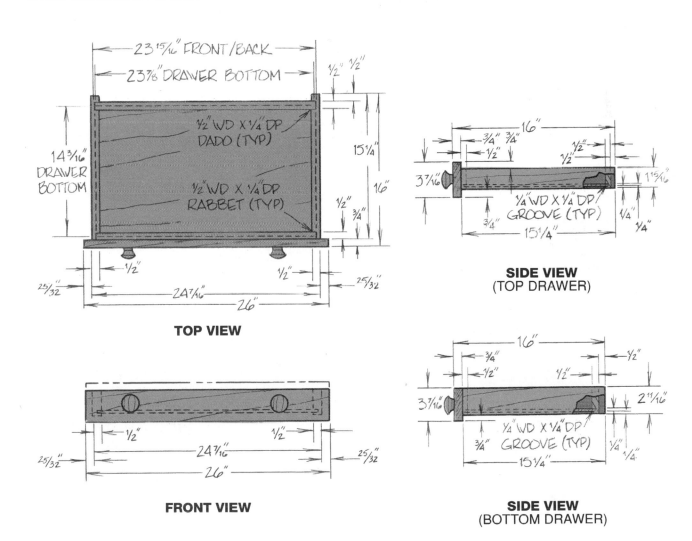

TOP VIEW

SIDE VIEW
(TOP DRAWER)

FRONT VIEW

SIDE VIEW
(BOTTOM DRAWER)

DRAWER

14 Cut the door joinery.

The doors are assembled with haunched mortises and tenons, and mounted to the case with piano hinges. Cut the following joints:

- ³/₄″-wide, ³/₁₆″-deep rabbets in the inside faces of the outside door stiles, as shown in *Section D,* to accommodate the piano hinges
- ³/₈″-wide, ³/₈″-deep rabbets in the adjoining edges of the inside door stiles so the doors will lap each other

- ¼″-wide, ³/₈″-deep grooves in the inside edges of all door stiles and rails
- ¼″-wide, 1″-deep (as measured from the inside edges), 1¼″-long mortises in the stiles, ³/₈″ from either end, as shown in the *Door Joinery Detail*
- ¼″-thick, 1″-long tenons on the ends of the rails

Using a band saw or a dovetail saw, notch the tenons to create a "haunch," and fit them to their mortises.

15 Assemble and mount the doors.

Finish sand the door parts. Assemble the rails and stiles with glue, inserting the tenons in the mortises. Remember that the rabbets on the left and right inside door stiles must face in *opposite* directions, as shown in *Section D.* As you assemble the doors, slide the panels in place but do *not* glue them. Let them float in their grooves. Sand all joints clean and flush, then attach door pulls to the inside stiles.

Mount the doors on the case with piano hinges so the rabbet in the right inside door stile laps over the left. Install a catch inside the case for the right door.

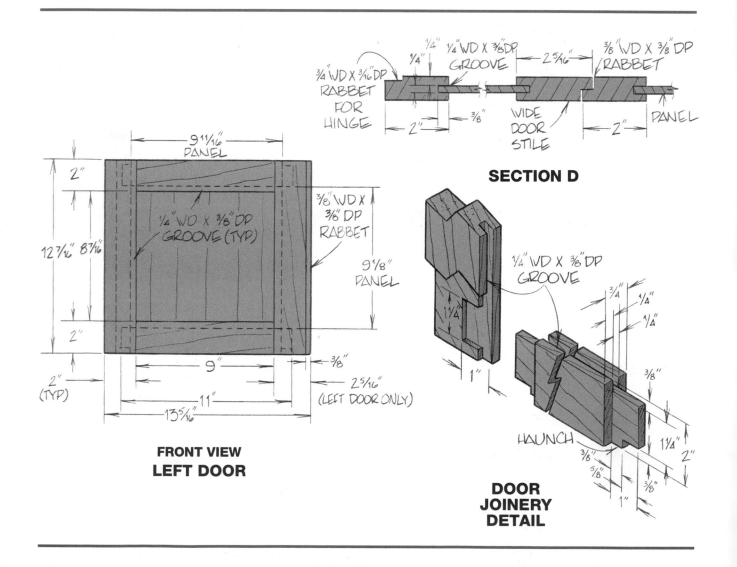

SECTION D

**FRONT VIEW
LEFT DOOR**

**DOOR
JOINERY
DETAIL**

16 Cut the shapes of the fence parts.
Lay out the cutouts in the fence and fence base. Cut these shapes with a band saw or saber saw.

Also, miter the back top corner of the four outside braces, as shown in the *Fence/Side View*. Sand the sawed edges.

17 Drill the fence parts.
Drill $5/16''$-diameter holes through the fence base, as shown in the *Fence/Top View*. These holes must be spaced precisely the same as the slots in the worktable. Also drill or cut a $2\frac{1}{4}''$-diameter hole in the dust collector back, as shown in the *Fence/Front View* and *Section E*. This large hole will accept a standard-size nozzle on the hose of a shop vacuum, so you can collect sawdust while you're routing.

18 Assemble and mount the fence.
Finish sand the fence parts. Assemble them with glue and screws. As you did when assembling the case, counterbore and countersink each of the screws, then cover the heads with wooden plugs. Sand the plugs and the joints clean and flush.

To mount the fence, insert carriage bolts through the worktable slots from the bottom, then through the $5/16''$-diameter holes in the fence base. Put flat washers over the ends of the bolts, then secure them with wing nuts. To move the fence, loosen the wing nuts, slide it to the desired position, and tighten the nuts.

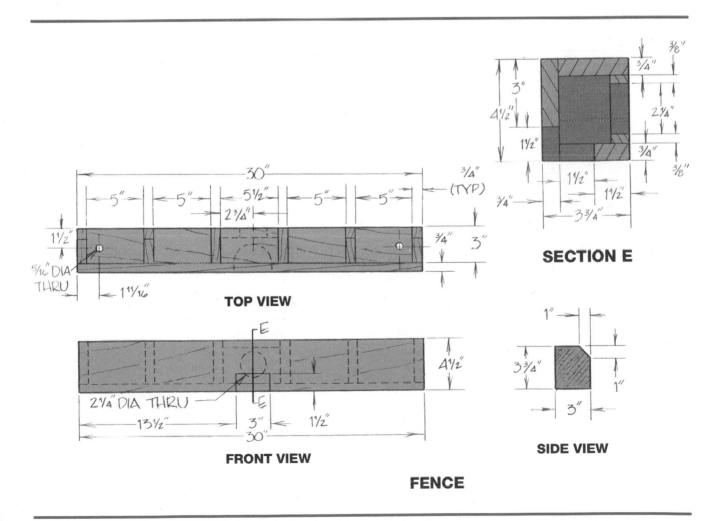

TOP VIEW

SECTION E

FRONT VIEW

SIDE VIEW

FENCE

19

Mount the router. Using a saber saw, cut a sheet of ³/₈″-thick acrylic plastic to fit the cutout in the worktable. This will make a mounting plate for the router. Drill a 3″-diameter hole through the center of this plate, as shown in the *Top View*.

Remove the base from your router. Place the acrylic plate on the workbench and center the router on top of it. Mark the position of the base mounting holes. Remove the router, then drill mounting holes in the acrylic. Countersink these holes on the top surface. Also drill and countersink ³/₁₆″-diameter pilot holes at the corners of the plate to mount it to the worktable.

Mount the acrylic plate to the worktable with flathead wood screws. The top surface of the acrylic must be precisely flush with that of the worktable, and the screws should be slightly below the surface. Using the same bolts that hold the base to your router, attach the router to the underside of the acrylic plate. Once again, the heads of these bolts should be slightly below the surface of the plastic.

20

Finish the router cabinet. Remove the doors, drawers, router, acrylic plate, and all hardware from the case. Apply a finish to the wooden parts. Coat all sides of the cabinet, inside and out, top and bottom. Buff the finish with wax, and wax the surface of the worktable. Finally, replace the doors, drawers, plate, and other hardware.

21

Install a switch, plug, and power cord. For safety and convenience, install a switch under the worktable to quickly cut off the power to the router. Turn the cabinet upside down and attach a metal electrical box to the table. Place it near the front edge, toward either the left or the right side (depending on whether you're right- or left-handed).

Remove a knockout from the back of the box, install a box connector in the opening, and insert a grounded appliance cord through the connector. Strip the wires and attach them to a combination switch and outlet. (See Figure 6.) Note that there are two sides to the switch/outlet. One side has a silver screw and a brass screw. The other has two brass screws bridged by a break-off tab. There will also be a green screw for the ground. Attach the black (hot) wire to the brass screw on the *opposite* side from the tab. Attach the white wire to the silver screw, and the green (ground) wire to the ground screw. Do *not* remove the break-off tab, unless otherwise instructed by the manufacturer.

Install the switch/outlet in the electrical box, pulling any excess cord out through the connector. Tighten the connector's cable clamps, and install the outlet plate. Run the cord out through the electrical access hole in the back of the cabinet, and attach a grounded plug to the cord if it does not already have one.

Warning: Before you plug the cord into a wall outlet, check the electrical connections with a circuit tester.

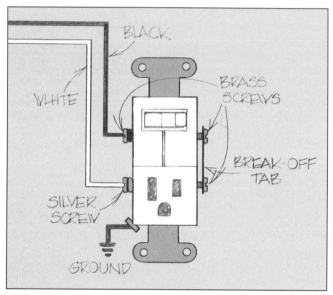

6/When you install the switch/outlet, attach the wires as shown so the switch will control the out-let. Do **not** remove the break-off tab unless instructed by the manufacturer.

Step-by-Step: Making Haunched Mortises and Tenons

The doors on workshop furniture see plenty of use and abuse — far more than ordinary furniture doors. Weighty equipment and materials bang into the doors of a workshop cabinet more often than you'd like to think. For this reason, the doors should be made as strong as possible.

Among the strongest joints you can use for assembling frame-and-panel doors is the haunched mortise-and-tenon joint. It is also among the simplest to make, particularly if you're using the Router Mortising Jig shown in this book.

1

Using a straight bit, rout grooves in the **inside** edges of all the rails and stiles. Feed the wood so the rotation of the bit keeps the wood pressed against the worktable.

2

Adjust the bit so that it cuts two to three times deeper than the grooves you just routed. (For instance, if the grooves were ⅜" deep, adjust the bit to cut ¾"–1" deep.) Do not change the height of the bit above the worktable.

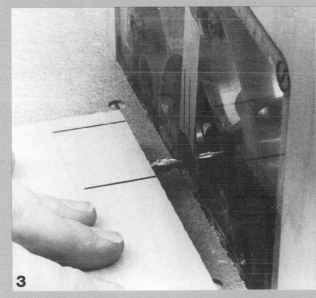

3

Carefully mark the beginning and end of each mortise on the faces of the stiles. Feed each stile into the bit sideways, drilling a series of overlapping holes to rough out each mortise.

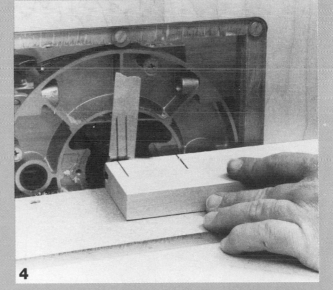

4

After roughing out the mortise, hold a stile against the fence and feed it back and forth to clean up the edges of the mortises. Be careful not to elongate the mortises — don't cut past the marks.

(continued)

Step-by-Step: Making Haunched Mortises and Tenons — Continued

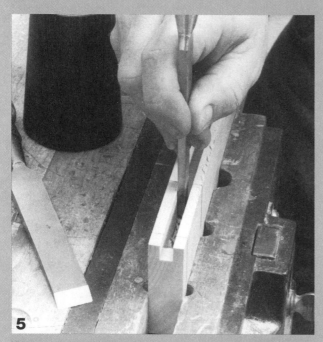

5

Square the blind end of each mortise with a hand chisel. A mortising chisel works best for this task.

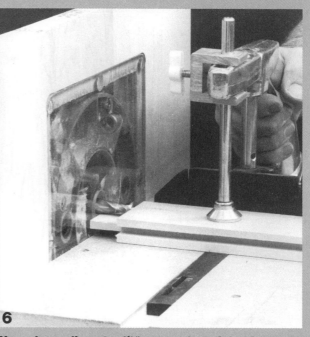

6

Use a large diameter (½″ or more) straight bit to make the tenons on the ends of the rails. Cut away the waste on one side of the rail, then turn it over and cut the other side. The tenons must be long enough to reach the bottom of the mortises. They must be as thick as the mortises are wide.

7

Using a band saw or a dovetail saw, notch the outside edges of the tenons so they fit the mortises and grooves. This notch is called the "haunch."

8

When the tenon is properly fitted to a mortise, the outside edge of the rail will be flush with the end of the stile.

Sandpaper Dispenser

S andpaper has an annoying tendency to curl up if you keep it around your shop for any length of time. The paper is coated on one side with an adhesive that secures the grit. The uncoated side absorbs moisture faster, swells, and causes the paper to curl. Curled sandpaper can be difficult to mount in machines and sanding blocks.

There are three ways to keep sandpaper from curling: (1) You can coat the open side of the paper with varnish or lacquer immediately after you buy it; (2) you can move your shop to the Arizona desert, where there is little humidity; or (3) you can build this ingenious sandpaper dispenser.

Larry Callahan of West Milton, Ohio, designed this project. As with many great ideas, it's absurdly simple. The dispenser is a small chest of drawers, each drawer just big enough to store full-size sheets of sandpaper. Each drawer also has a heavy lid which keeps the paper from curling. What could be easier?

Materials List

FINISHED DIMENSIONS

PARTS

A.	Sides (2)	$3/4'' \times 9^{13}/_{16}'' \times 12^3/_4''$
B.	Top	$3/4'' \times 13^1/_2'' \times 13^1/_2''$
C.	Bottom	$3/4'' \times 10^1/_2'' \times 12^1/_4''$
D.	Back	$1/2'' \times 9^{13}/_{16}'' \times 11''$
E.	Guides (12)	$1/4'' \times 1/2'' \times 12''$
F.	Drawer fronts (6)	$1/2'' \times 1^7/_{16}'' \times 10^7/_{16}''$
G.	Drawer sides (12)	$1/2'' \times 1^7/_{16}'' \times 12''$
H.	Drawer backs (6)	$1/2'' \times 1^7/_{16}'' \times 9^7/_{16}''$
J.	Drawer bottoms (6)	$1/8'' \times 9^7/_8'' \times 11^{11}/_{16}''$
K.	Lids (6)	$1/4'' \times 9^3/_8'' \times 11^3/_{16}''$

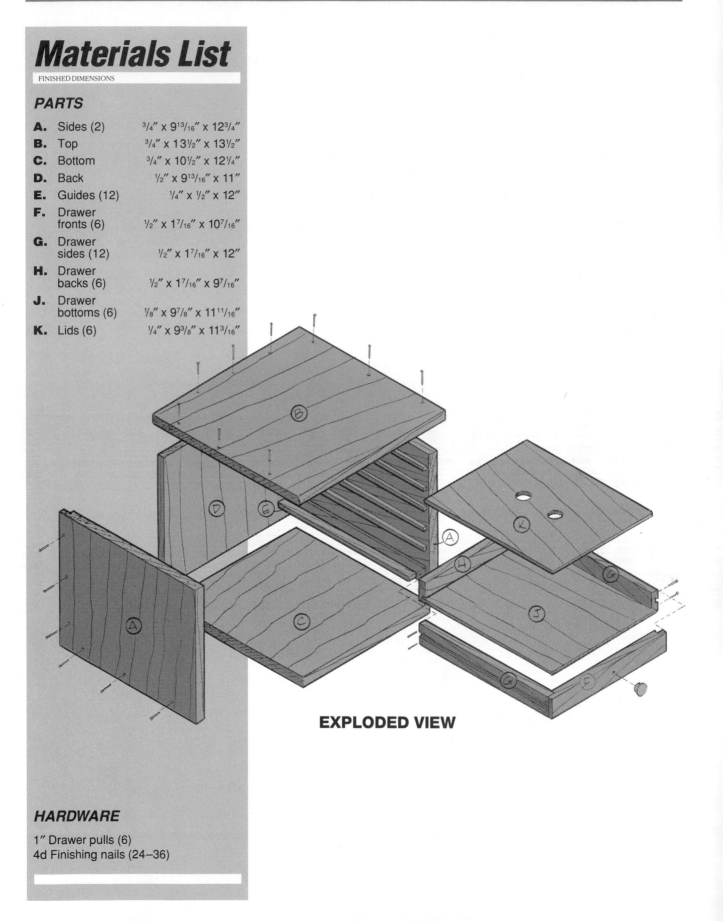

EXPLODED VIEW

HARDWARE

1″ Drawer pulls (6)
4d Finishing nails (24–36)

1 Determine the size of the dispenser.

The dispenser shown has six drawers, one each for 50#, 80#, 100#, 120#, 150#, and 180# sandpapers. Depending on the sort of woodworking you do, this may be too many or too few drawers. Decide how many drawers you need, then adjust the size of the case to hold them.

2 Select the stock and cut the parts to size.

To make this project as designed, you need about 10 board feet of 4/4 (four-quarters) stock, a 2′ x 4′ sheet of ¼″ hardboard, and a 2′ x 4′ sheet of ⅛″ hardboard. You can use almost any stock, but make the drawer sides and guides — the sliding parts — from a very hard wood, such as birch, maple, or oak. These woods wear better than softer species. Also, choose *tempered* hardboard — it's slightly denser and wears better than the untempered variety.

When you have gathered the materials, cut the parts to the sizes needed.

3 Cut the joinery for the case and drawers.

Both the case and the drawers are joined with simple rabbets, dadoes, and grooves. Using a dado cutter or a router, cut these joints:

- ½″-wide, ¼″-deep rabbets in the back edges of the sides, as shown in the *Side Layout,* to hold the back
- ½″-wide, ¼″-deep rabbets in the ends of the drawer fronts, as shown in the *Drawer/Top View,* to hold the drawer sides
- 5⁄16″-wide, ¼″-deep grooves in the drawer sides to fit over the drawer guides
- ¼″-wide, ¼″-deep dadoes in the sides to hold the drawer guides
- ⅛″-wide, ¼″-deep grooves in the drawer fronts, sides, and backs, to hold the drawer bottoms

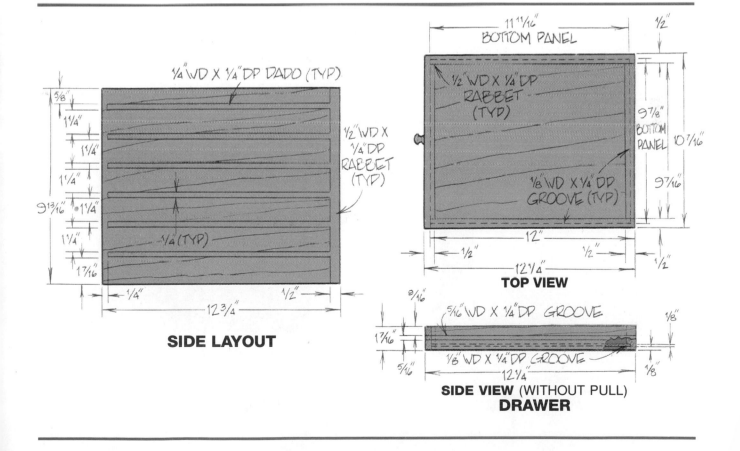

SIDE LAYOUT

TOP VIEW

SIDE VIEW (WITHOUT PULL)
DRAWER

4

Assemble the case. Finish sand the top, bottom, sides, and back. Glue the *first 2″–3″* of the drawer guides in the side dadoes. Do *not* glue the entire length of the drawer guides; this would restrict the movement of the sides as they expand and contract.

When the glue dries, assemble the top, bottom, sides, and back with glue and finishing nails. Sand the joints clean and flush, then set the heads of the nails.

5

Assemble the drawers. Finish sand the drawer fronts. Assemble the drawer fronts, backs, and sides with glue and nails. Slide the bottoms in place as you assemble the drawers, but do *not* glue them. Let them float in their grooves.

When the glue dries, sand all joints clean and flush. Set the nails, then attach drawer pulls to the drawer fronts.

Note: Spin the nails in partway to avoid splitting the sides.

6

Fit the drawers to the case. Slide the drawers in the case, fitting the grooves in the sides of the drawers over the drawer guides. Test the sliding action. If any drawer sticks or binds, deepen or enlarge the drawer side grooves with a scraper. (See Figure 1.) If any drawer rubs on another drawer, sand or plane some stock from the top or bottom edges of either drawer.

1/To scrape a small area — such as the grooves in the drawer sides — make a small scraper from any flat, stiff metal scrap. Some woodworkers cut up old scrapers to make smaller ones. Grind the edge of the small scraper square and burnish it to create a burr.

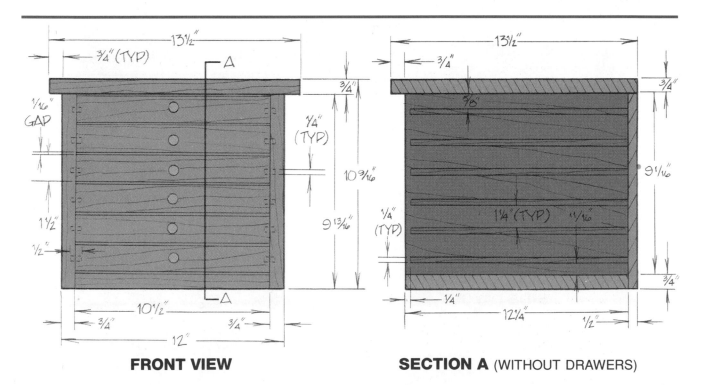

FRONT VIEW   **SECTION A** (WITHOUT DRAWERS)

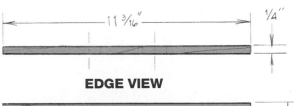

EDGE VIEW

7

Make and fit the lids. Drill 1″-diameter finger holes in the lids, as shown in the *Lid Layout.* (See Figure 2.) Then lay the lids in the drawers. They should fit with about ¹⁄₁₆″ of slop all around the perimeter. If not, sand their edges until they fit properly.

2/When drilling the finger holes, stack the lids on top of each other, tape them together so they won't shift, then drill holes through the entire stack.

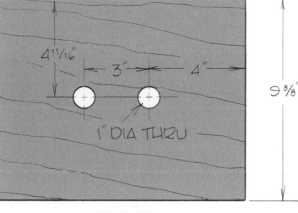

TOP VIEW

LID LAYOUT

8

Finish the dispenser. Remove the drawers and lids from the case. Do any necessary touch-up sanding, then apply a finish to the case and drawer fronts. Finish both the inside *and* outside of the case — this will keep it from warping. Rub a little paraffin wax on the drawer guides to help the drawers slide smoothly, then replace the drawers and lids.

TRY THIS! To help tear sandpaper sheets quickly, attach a worn-out hacksaw blade to the edge of the sandpaper dispenser's top. To cut a sheet, hold it flat on the dispenser with part of it hanging over the blade. Tear down — the teeth will cut the paper cleanly.

Work Cart

No matter how carefully you plan your shop, it seems your tools aren't always where you need them. There are two ways to solve this problem. You can buy duplicates of each important tool and keep them at various locations around the shop. Or you can get along with the tools you already own by bringing them to the job in a *work cart*.

This particular cart is the invention of Judy Ditmer, proprietor of Heartwood in Tipp City, Ohio. Judy is a professional turner, and she uses the cart to carry her turning tools between two lathes. The cart offers space for small tools, jigs, and templates. Two foldout trays on either side of the cart increase the working area, so the cart doubles as an auxiliary workbench. A power strip provides electricity for portable power tools. ●

Materials List

FINISHED DIMENSIONS

PARTS

A. Long legs (2) $1\frac{1}{2}'' \times 1\frac{1}{2}'' \times 48''$

B. Short legs (2) $1\frac{1}{2}'' \times 1\frac{1}{2}'' \times 36''$

C. Supports (2) $1\frac{1}{2}'' \times 1\frac{1}{2}'' \times 28''$

D. Large trays* (3) $\frac{3}{4}'' \times 17\frac{1}{4}'' \times 17\frac{1}{4}''$

E. Folding trays* (2) $\frac{3}{4}'' \times 15\frac{1}{4}'' \times 17\frac{1}{4}''$

F. Small tray* $\frac{3}{4}'' \times 10\frac{1}{2}'' \times 21\frac{3}{4}''$

G. Large tray fronts/backs (6) $\frac{3}{4}'' \times 2\frac{1}{4}'' \times 18''$

H. Folding tray fronts/backs (4) $\frac{3}{4}'' \times 2\frac{1}{4}'' \times 16''$

J. Large and folding tray sides (10) $\frac{3}{4}'' \times 2\frac{1}{4}'' \times 16\frac{1}{2}''$

K. Small tray front/back (2) $\frac{3}{4}'' \times 1\frac{1}{2}'' \times 22\frac{1}{2}''$

L. Small tray sides (2) $\frac{3}{4}'' \times 1\frac{1}{2}'' \times 9\frac{3}{4}''$

M. Stops (2) $\frac{3}{4}'' \times 1\frac{1}{2}'' \times 1\frac{1}{2}''$

N. Braces (2) $\frac{3}{4}'' \times 1\frac{1}{2}'' \times 20\frac{5}{8}''$

P. Spacers (4) $1'' \times 1\frac{1}{2}'' \times 1\frac{1}{2}''$

*Make these from plywood.

HARDWARE

$4'' \times 1\frac{1}{2}''$ Butt hinges and mounting screws (6)

#10 x $1\frac{1}{4}''$ Flathead wood screws (72–84)

$\frac{3}{8}''$ Screw plugs (44)

2" Casters (4)

EXPLODED VIEW

1

Select the stock and cut the parts to size. To make this project, you need about 10 board feet of 4/4 (four-quarters) hardwood stock, 8 board feet of 8/4 (eight-quarters) stock, and one sheet (4' x 8') of ¾" cabinet-grade plywood. The work cart shown is made from birch and birch-veneer plywood, but you could also use oak or maple. If the cart is intended for light duty, you can also use soft woods.

When you have purchased the stock, cut all the parts to the sizes shown in the Materials List, except the folding tray fronts. For these, cut a single board, ¾" x 4⅝" x 16".

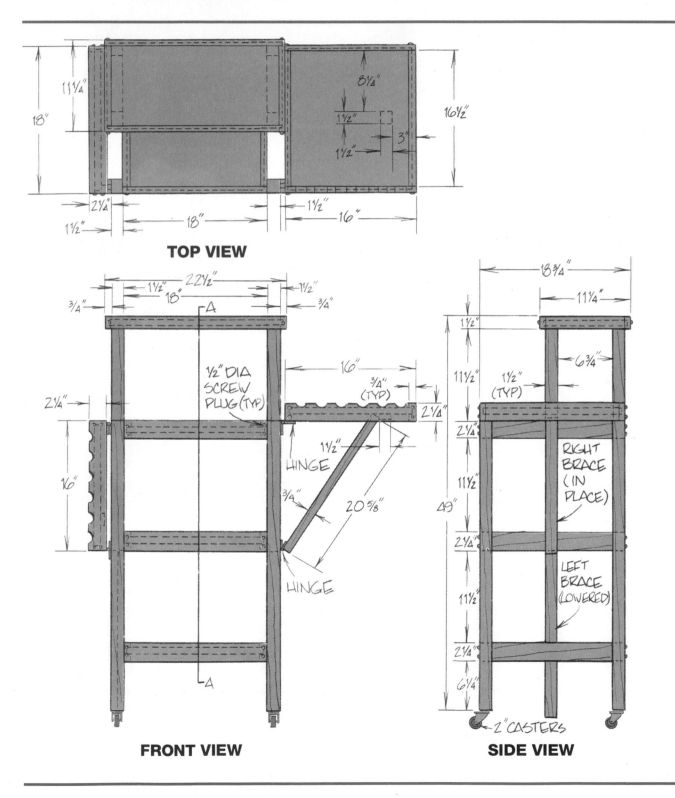

TOP VIEW

FRONT VIEW

SIDE VIEW

2 Cut the scallops in the folding tray fronts.

The folding tray fronts are scalloped to help organize chisels and similar tools. This makes the tools easier to reach and keeps them from rolling around. To make the scallops, mark the center of the stock, then drill 1½″-diameter holes through it, spaced every 2½″, as shown in the *Folding Tray Layout*. Rip the stock in half to make two pieces, each 2½″ wide. (See Figure 1.) Then rip ¼″ from the width of each piece, making them 2¼″ wide.

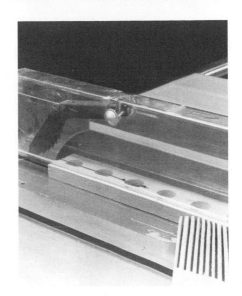

1/After drilling a line of evenly spaced 1½″-diameter holes through the folding tray front stock, rip it in half. This will create two pieces, each with half-round scallops in one edge.

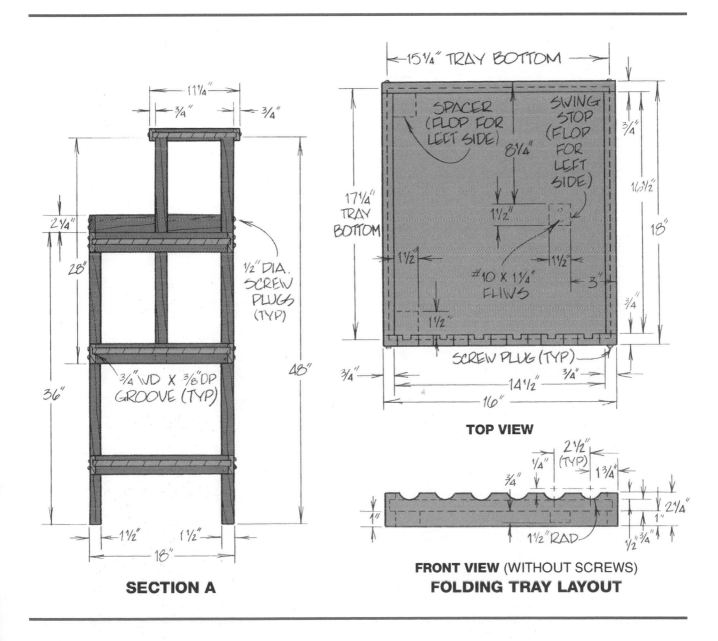

SECTION A

TOP VIEW

FRONT VIEW (WITHOUT SCREWS)
FOLDING TRAY LAYOUT

3

Cut the tray joinery. The trays rest in ¾"-wide, ⅜"-deep grooves in the tray fronts, backs, and sides. The grooves in the sides are open on both ends, but those in the fronts and backs of the top tray and folding trays are *double-blind* — they stop ⅜" before each end. Cut all the grooves with a router and a 1¾" straight bit. Square the blind ends with a chisel. (See Figures 2 and 3.)

2/To rout a groove in narrow stock, clamp the board to your workbench between two boards the same thickness as the one you want to rout. This will provide more support for the router. Use an edge guide to direct the router. If you're making a blind groove, stop routing before you reach the end of the board.

3/Square the blind ends of the grooves with a chisel. If you have one, use a mortising chisel.

4

Drill the legs for casters. Drill holes in the bottom ends of both the long and short legs, to hold swivel casters. The diameter of these holes will depend on the make of the casters.

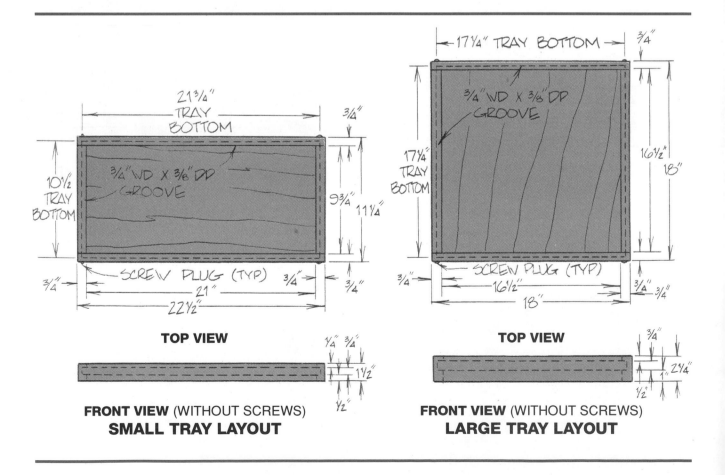

Small tray layout: 21¾" TRAY BOTTOM · 10½ TRAY BOTTOM · ¾" WD X ⅜" DP GROOVE · ¾" · 9¾" · 11¼" · ¾" · SCREW PLUG (TYP) · ¾" · ¾" · 21" · 22½" · ¼" · ¾" · 1½" · ½"

TOP VIEW

FRONT VIEW (WITHOUT SCREWS)
SMALL TRAY LAYOUT

Large tray layout: 17¼" TRAY BOTTOM · ¾" · ¾" WD X ⅜" DP GROOVE · 17¼" TRAY BOTTOM · 16½" · 18" · ¾" · SCREW PLUG (TYP) · 16½" · ¾" · ¾" · 18" · ¾" · 1" · 2¼" · ½"

TOP VIEW

FRONT VIEW (WITHOUT SCREWS)
LARGE TRAY LAYOUT

5

Assemble the trays. Finish sand the parts of the work cart, being careful not to round over any adjoining edges or ends. Then glue the trays, fronts, backs, and sides together. After the glue dries, sand the joints clean and flush. Reinforce the corners with flathead wood screws. Counterbore *and* countersink the heads of the screws.

6

Assemble the large trays, small tray, legs, and supports. Mark the positions of the trays on all the legs and supports. Lay out the right long leg, right short leg, and right support on a flat surface. Attach the top and middle large trays to these parts by driving screws through the sides of the trays and into the legs or supports, as shown in the *Tray-to-Leg Joinery Detail.* Countersink the heads of the screws. Attach the bottom large tray in the same manner.

Lay out the left legs and support. Turn the cart assembly over on its left side, position it over these parts, and attach it to them. Once again, countersink the heads of the screws.

Stand the cart up and attach the small tray to it. Drive screws down through the small tray into the top ends of the legs and supports. Again, countersink the heads of the screws.

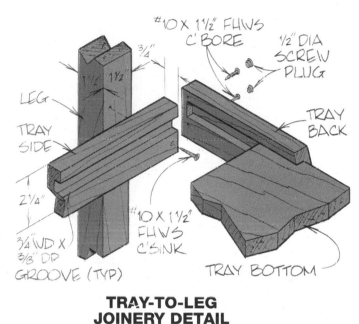

TRAY-TO-LEG JOINERY DETAIL

7

Mount the folding trays. To mount the hinges on the folding trays, attach spacers to the tray bottoms for something to drive the screws into. Glue the spacers in the inside corners. The bottom surface of the spacers should be flush with the bottom edges of the tray sides.

Attach the braces to the bottom ends of the supports with hinges. Then mount the folding trays to the long and short legs with hinges. When mounted and folded *down,* the inside sides of each folding tray should be flush with the top edge of the top large tray, as shown in the *Front View.*

With a helper, lift one folding tray until it's horizontal, using a bubble level to determine when it's parallel with the ground. Then lift the brace until it touches the bottom surface of the tray. Put the stop in place and mark its position. Fold the brace back down and attach the stop to the bottom of the tray with glue and screws. Repeat for the other tray.

When you need to put a tray up, simply lift it slightly above horizontal, bring the brace up into position, and let the tray settle until the stop is resting against the end of the brace.

8

Finish the cart. Remove the folding trays, braces, and all the hardware from the cart. Glue screw plugs in all the counterbores to hide the heads of the flathead screws. Do any necessary touch-up sanding, then apply a finish to the completed work cart, folding trays, and braces. Apply several coats of wax on top of the finish to keep glue from sticking to the wood, then replace the braces and folding trays. Mount the casters in the bottom ends of the legs and, if you wish, attach a power strip to the bottom surface of the large top tray.

Plywood Cutting Tables

Cutting a full sheet of plywood presents a dilemma in most home workshops. The sheet is too big and too heavy to handle safely on a table saw. If you lay it across sawhorses and use a circular saw, the horses may not provide enough support. They may allow the sheet to flex and bow so the blade binds as you approach the end of the cut. You could get plenty of support by laying the plywood on the floor, on top of a scrap sheet. But then you can't clamp a straightedge to the plywood to guide your saw. Unless your hand is extremely steady, the long cuts are likely to be slightly uneven.

What's the solution? Make a set of *plywood cutting tables*. These tables provide adequate support for the plywood *and* they raise the plywood off the floor slightly so you can clamp a straightedge to it.

The tables shown can be made quickly and inexpensively from construction lumber. There are two tables in the set. Use one table to cut partial sheets, and both to cut full sheets. You can also use these as assembly tables to raise a large project off the floor slightly. To store the tables, fit them together bottom side to bottom side so the legs interlock, and lean them against a wall.

Materials List

FINISHED DIMENSIONS

PARTS

For Two Tables

A.	Sides (4)	1½″ x 3½″ x 57″
B.	Ends/stringers (10)	1½″ x 3½″ x 54″
C.	Rails (6)	1½″ x 1½″ x 57″
D.	Legs (10)	1½″ x 3½″ x 7″

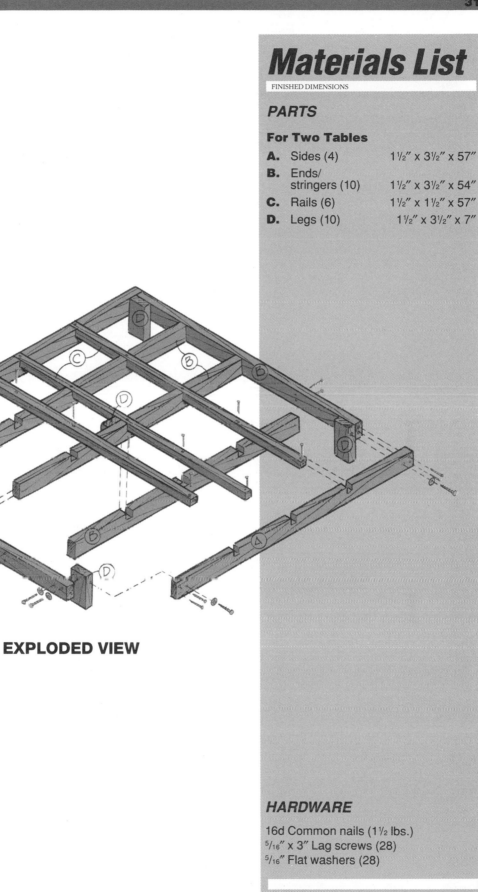

EXPLODED VIEW

HARDWARE

16d Common nails (1½ lbs.)
5/16″ x 3″ Lag screws (28)
5/16″ Flat washers (28)

1 **_Select the stock and cut the parts to size._** To make this project, you'll need nine 2 x 4s, 10' long. Select straight stock — you want the tables to be as flat as possible. Cut two of the 2 x 4s in half to make four pieces about 60" long, and rip three of these pieces into 2 x 2s (1½" x 1½"). Then cut all the parts to the sizes shown in the Materials List.

2 **_Cut the notches in the sides and stringers._** The rails rest in 1½"-wide, 1½"-deep notches in the sides and stringers. To make these notches, line up all the sides and stringers, face to face and top edge up, on your workbench. Make sure the ends of all the sides and the ends of all the stringers are flush. Position the sides so their ends overhang the stringers by 1½" on each end. Clamp all the sides and stringers together with bar clamps to keep them from shifting.

Measure and mark the locations of the notches on one side of a stringer, then transfer these marks across the other parts with a carpenter's square.

Adjust a circular saw to cut to a depth of 1½", then cut the faces of the notches, sawing across all the sides and stringers. (See Figure 1.) Using a wide chisel, knock out the waste in the notches. (See Figure 2.) When you remove the bar clamps, the notches in all the sides and stringers will be cut to exactly the same depth and width. Furthermore, they'll be spaced precisely the same.

1/Clamp the sides and stringers together to saw the notches in all the parts at the same time. After cutting the faces, saw several kerfs through the waste to make it easier to remove.

2/With the sides and stringers still clamped together, remove the waste from the notches with a chisel. Cut down to the bottoms of the saw kerfs.

3 **_Assemble the table frame._** Assemble the sides, ends, and stringers with 16d nails. Lay the rails in the notches to make a grid. The top edges of the rails, stringers, and sides should all be flush. If not, cut the notches deeper or raise the rails with shims. When the parts are flush, secure the rails with nails.

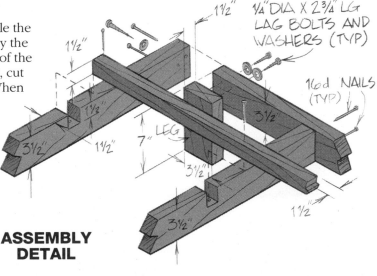

ASSEMBLY DETAIL

4 **Attach the legs.** Lay one of the table grids upside-down on the floor of the workshop. Using lag screws, attach a leg to each of the four corners and to the left side of the middle stringer, as shown in the *Top View*.

Put the other table grid right side up on top of the first, fitting it over the upturned legs. Attach legs to the second grid near the four corners and to the right side of the middle stringer, as shown. This second set of legs shouldn't touch or interfere with the first set.

To use the tables, take them apart and stand them both right side up, on their legs. For extra stability, clamp the ends of the tables together. When you want to store them, put them back together so the legs interlock.

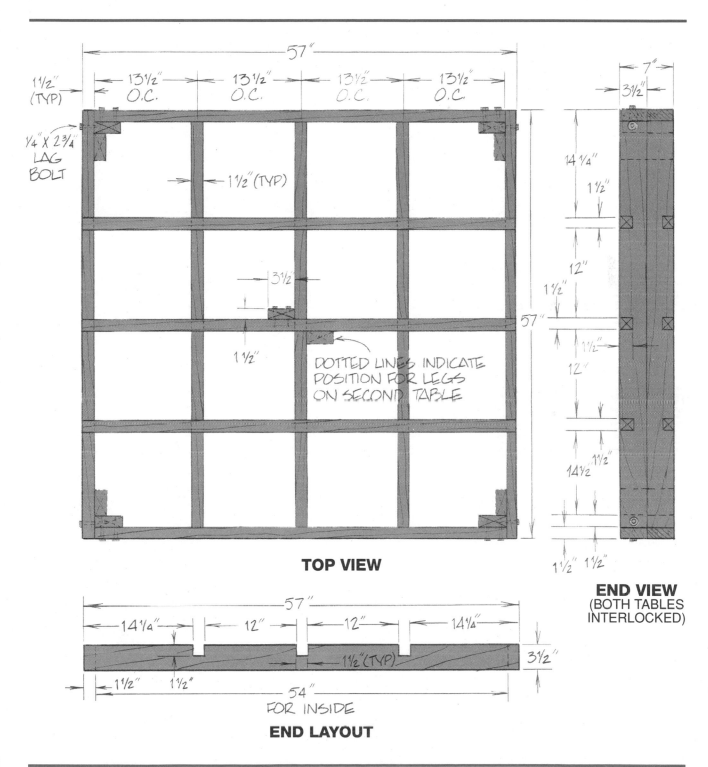

TOP VIEW

END VIEW
(BOTH TABLES
INTERLOCKED)

END LAYOUT

Dust Control Cart

Sawdust is a major health problem in every woodworking shop, but it's particularly acute in small home workshops. Most of these shops are in garages or basements and are not well ventilated. The air quickly fills with dust particles as you work and before long, you're breathing sawdust.

In a short time, you may feel physical discomfort — watery eyes, rashes, sneezing, and coughing. Longer periods of exposure can cause more serious problems such as respiratory distress and allergic reactions. Breathing sawdust may be extremely dangerous if you have asthma, emphysema, or other chronic respiratory disorders. It's also dangerous if you're working with a wood species known to generate *toxic* sawdust — boxwood, cedar, ebony, mahogany, rosewood, redwood, teak, and "outdoor" lumber that has been treated with a chemical preservative. Many woodworkers also experience health problems after breathing sawdust from wood with high concentrations of tannic acid, such as oak and walnut.

To avoid these problems, make sure your shop is properly ventilated. Change the filters on your air conditioner and furnace frequently. You may also want to build this simple dust

control cart. It uses an ordinary box fan to pull the air in your shop through two washable furnace filters, removing the larger dust particles. It will also remove fine saw-

dust if you sandwich a sheet of loosely woven cotton muslin (available at any fabric store) between the two filters.

This dust control cart also serves as a work cart.

Roll it to wherever you're working, then rest small tools and materials on it. Or mount a tension lamp in the hole in the worktable, and use it as a portable worklight.

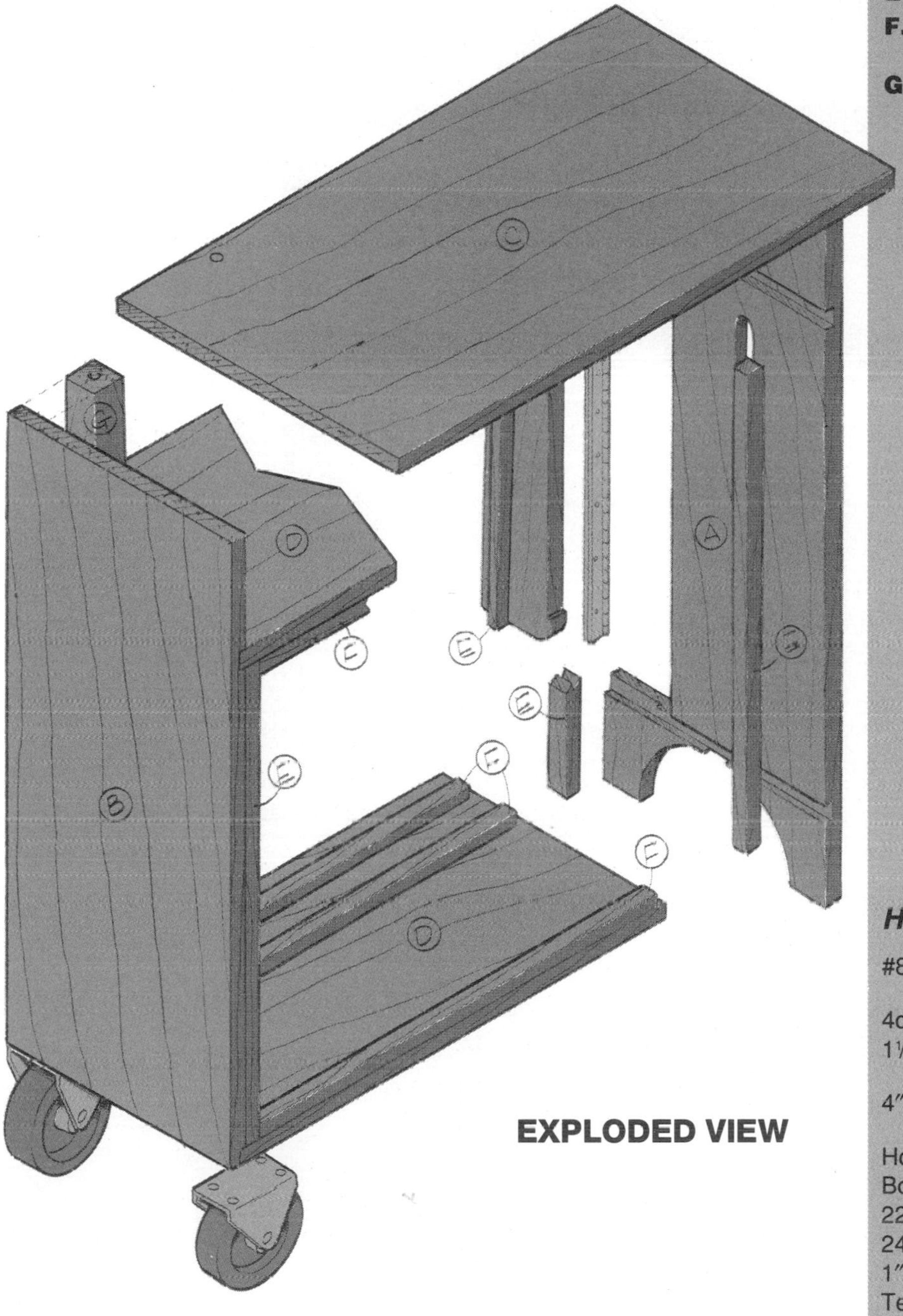

Materials List

FINISHED DIMENSIONS

PARTS

A. Long side $3/4'' \times 12'' \times 33\frac{1}{2}''$
B. Short side $3/4'' \times 12'' \times 29\frac{1}{2}''$
C. Top $3/4'' \times 15'' \times 26\frac{1}{2}''$
D. Shelves (2) $3/4'' \times 12'' \times 22\frac{3}{4}''$
E. Vertical cleats (6) $3/4'' \times 3/4'' \times 22''$
F. Horizontal
   cleats (6) $3/4'' \times 3/4'' \times 20\frac{1}{2}''$
G. Worklight mount $1\frac{1}{2}'' \times 1\frac{1}{2}'' \times 6''$

HARDWARE

#8 x 1¼" Flathead wood screws
   (24–30)
4d Finishing nails (¼ lb.)
1½" x 20" Piano hinge and mounting
   screws
4" Fixed casters and mounting
   screws (2)
Hook-and-eye
Box fan
22" x 22" Washable furnace filters (2)
24" x 24" Cotton muslin — optional
1" Foam rubber (scrap)
Tension lamp — optional

EXPLODED VIEW

1 **Adjust the design of the cart, if necessary.** Many of the dimensions of this dust control cart depend on the size of the box fan that you install in it. Most box fans are 21″ or 22″ square, depending on the manufacturer, but purchase the fan and measure it before you build this project. If neces-

sary, change the dimensions of the cart to fit the fan. Also, determine the locations of the fan control access hole, the electrical cord hole, and the cleats.

Note: The fan shouldn't fit too tightly. Leave *at least* ⅛″ of play top to bottom and ½″ side to side.

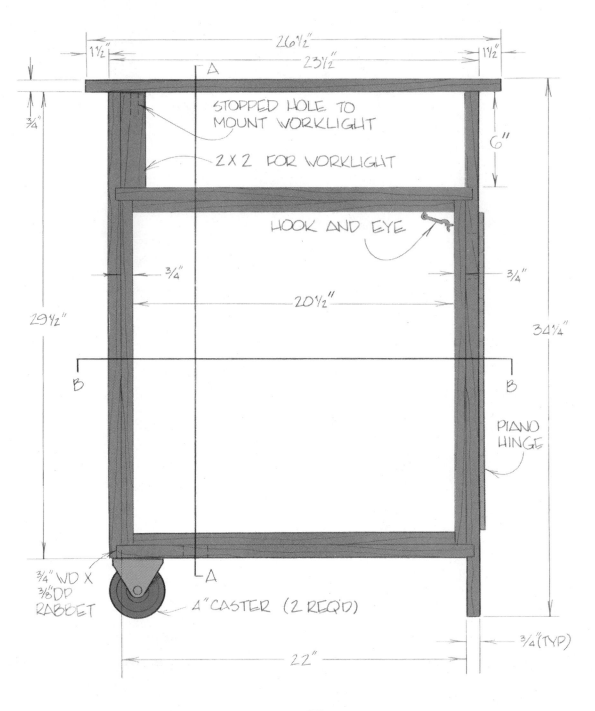

FRONT VIEW

2 Select the stock and cut the parts to size.
To make this project as designed, you need about 12 board feet of 4/4 (four-quarters) stock and a scrap of 8/4 (eight-quarters) stock. You may also use 3/4″ plywood instead of 4/4 lumber for the top, sides, and shelves, then trim the edges with thin pieces of hardwood. When you have selected the stock, plane and cut all the parts to size.

3 Cut the dadoes and rabbets in the sides.
The shelves are mounted in 3/4″-wide, 3/8″-deep dadoes and rabbets in the sides. Lay out these joints as shown in the *Long Side Layout,* then cut them with a dado cutter or router.

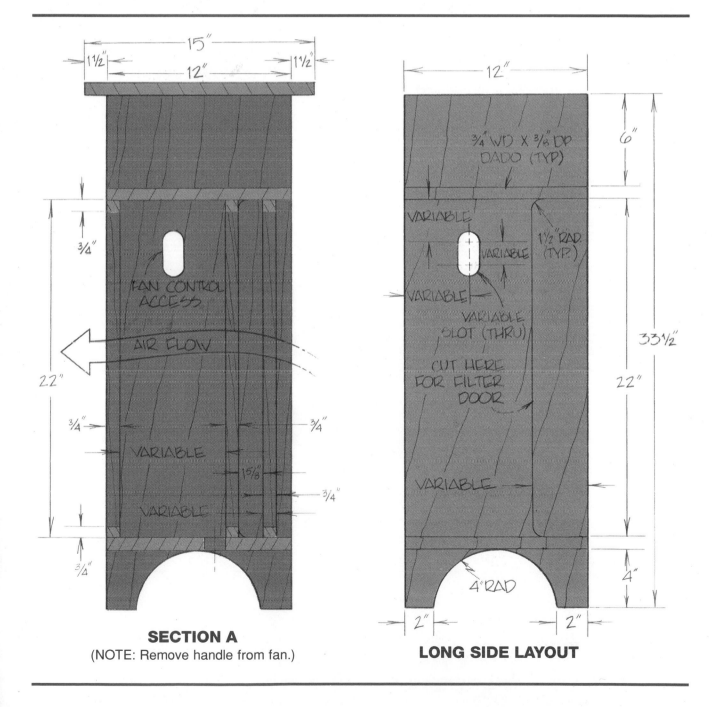

SECTION A
(NOTE: Remove handle from fan.)

LONG SIDE LAYOUT

4

Cut the feet, fan control access hole, and filter door. Lay out the shape of the fan control access hole on the long side. Also mark the filter door and the shape of the feet, as shown on the *Long Side Layout*. Drill a ½″-diameter hole through the waste where you want to start the cut for the fan control access hole. Cut the hole, door, and feet with a saber saw, and sand the sawed edges.

5

Drill the electrical cord hole. Measure and mark the location of a 1½″-diameter hole for the fan's electrical cord. Depending on the make of the fan, you may have to make this hole in the long side, short side, or bottom shelf.

6

Assemble the cart. Finish sand the parts, then assemble the sides, shelves, top, and work-light mount with glue and screws. Counterbore and countersink the screws, then cover the head with wood plugs. When the glue dries, sand all joints clean and flush. Sand the wooden plugs flush with the surface.

Attach the casters to the bottom shelf, near the short side, as shown in the *Front View*. Mortise the filter door for a piano hinge, then mount the door on the long side.

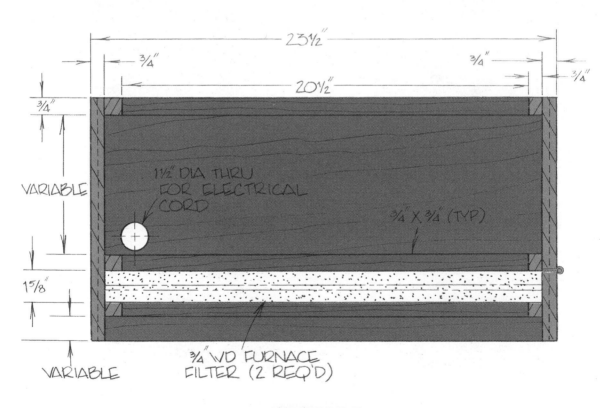

SECTION B

7

Mount the fan in the cart. Remove the handle and the control knob from the fan and slide the fan in place, inserting the electrical cord through its hole as you do so. Replace the control knob on its post. (On some fans, you may have to remove the entire switch to install the fan, then replace it when the fan is in place.)

Using flathead wood screws, attach the front set of four cleats to the inside surfaces of the cart, flush with the left-hand edges of the sides and shelves, as shown in *Section A*. Do *not* glue these cleats in place — you'll need to remove them later.

To keep the fan from rattling when you turn it on, stuff scraps of foam rubber between the fan and the inside surfaces of the cart. The front of the fan — the face that blows air *out* — should be placed snugly against the left-hand set of cleats.

Nail and glue a second set of cleats around the back of the fan, as shown in *Section A* and *Section B*.

8

Mount the filters in the cart. Nail and glue a vertical cleat to the short side and two horizontal cleats to the shelves, 1⅝" away from the cleats at the back of the fan, as shown in *Section A* and *Section B*. Also install a vertical cleat on the inside surface of the door. Open the door and slide two ¾"-thick furnace filters between the cleats. If you wish, sandwich a piece of cotton muslin between the two filters to remove fine dust particles. Install a hook-and-eye to keep the door closed.

9

Drill a hole for the worklight. If you wish to mount a tension lamp on your cart, measure the stud at the base of the lamp. Drill a stopped hole that matches the diameter and length of this stud through the top and into the worklight mount.

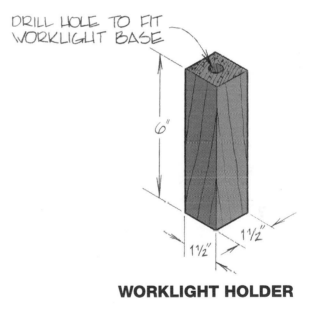

WORKLIGHT HOLDER

10

Finish the cart. Remove the front set of cleats and slide the fan out of the cart. Also remove the door and all the hardware. Do any necessary touch-up sanding, then apply a finish to the completed cart and door. Replace the door and the hardware. Also replace the fan and the front cleats. Once again, do *not* glue these cleats in place, in case you need to repair or replace the fan.

Work Island

The work seems easier and progresses faster when you can reach *all* sides of your project easily. To do this, however, you need a workbench in the middle of your shop that you can walk around — a *work island*.

The cabinet shown is an example of just such an island. There is no back; one side is the same as the other. There are doors on both sides and the drawers open from either side, so you can reach your tools no matter where you're standing. The work surface is large enough to hold most projects, but narrow enough that you can reach across it without stretching. Because the tabletop is narrow, you can use this bench in the middle of a relatively small shop.

This work island has several other features and options. With a set of casters, you can use it as an island or, when you need more floor space, place it against a wall. If you wish, you can mount vises on either side or end, and drill holes in the top for bench dogs and hold-downs. You can also attach an electrical outlet strip under the top to provide power for portable tools. ●

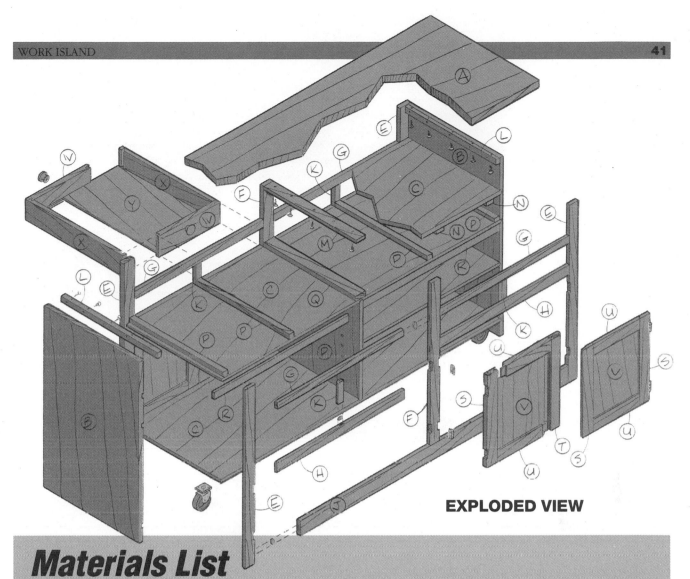

EXPLODED VIEW

Materials List

FINISHED DIMENSIONS

PARTS

A. Top   1¼″ x 25″ x 72″

B. Sides* (2)   ¾″ x 21½″ x 32¾″

C. Shelves* (3)   ¾″ x 21½″ x 59¼″

D. Divider*   ¾″ x 21½″ x 18⅛″

E. Left/right face frame stiles (4)   ¾″ x 2″ x 32¾″

F. Middle face frame stiles (2)   ¾″ x 2″ x 29¾″

G. Top face frame rails (4)   ¾″ x 1¼″ x 27″

H. Middle face frame rails (4)   ¾″ x 2″ x 27″

J. Bottom face frame rails (2)   ¾″ x 3″ x 56″

K. Mullions (4)   ¾″ x 1″ x 4″

L. End cleats (2)   ¾″ x ¾″ x 21½″

M. Middle cleat   ¾″ x 2″ x 21½″

N. Kickers (8)   ½″ x 2″ x 21½″

P. Left/right drawer guides (4)   ¾″ x 1″ x 21½″

Q. Middle drawer guide   ¾″ x 2″ x 21½″

R. Door stops (4)   ½″ x 1⅝″ x 28⅞″

S. Narrow door stiles (12)   ¾″ x 2″ x 16⅜″

T. Wide door stiles (4)   ¾″ x 2⅜″ x 16⅜″

U. Door rails (16)   ¾″ x 2″ x 11⁷⁄₁₆″

V. Door panels* (8)   ¼″ x 10⅛″ x 13¹⁄₁₆″

W. Drawer ends (8)   ¾″ x 3¹⁵⁄₁₆″ x 12¹⁵⁄₁₆″

X. Drawer sides (8)   ¾″ x 3¹⁵⁄₁₆″ x 22½″

Y. Drawer bottoms* (4)   ¼″ x 12⅛″ x 22³⁄₁₆″

*Make these from plywood.

HARDWARE

1½″ x 2½″ Butt hinges and mounting screws (16)

1½″ Door/drawer pulls (24)

Door catches (8)

#00 Plates (32)

#20 Plates (28)

#8 x 1¼″ Flathead wood screws (84–96)

4″ Swivel casters (4)

1

Determine the size of the island. Both the length and the width of the island can be adjusted to fit your shop — simply make various parts longer or wider. Measure the space available in your shop, allowing adequate walkways (at least 24″ wide) all around the island. Determine the overall dimensions of the island, then adjust the dimensions of the parts.

Note: Don't make the island wider than 30″. Unless you're very tall (or have unusually long arms), you won't be able to reach across it.

2

Select the stock and cut the parts to size. To make this project, you need about 22 board feet of 6/4 (six-quarters) hardwood, 32 board feet of 4/4 (four-quarters) hardwood, two 4′ x 8′ sheets of ¾″ cabinet-grade plywood, and one sheet of ¼″ cabinet-grade plywood. Select a hard, durable wood to make this project, such as maple, birch, or oak. The work island shown is made from maple, birch, and birch-veneer plywood.

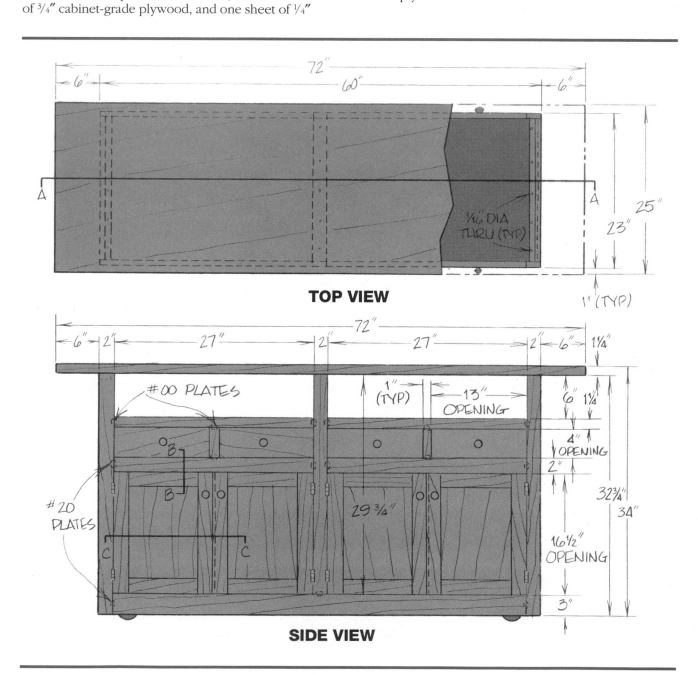

TOP VIEW

SIDE VIEW

If you wish, you can substitute a laminated maple countertop for the 6/4 hardwood. This will save you the time and trouble of making a work surface by gluing the boards edge to edge and then having the wide stock planed flat. These wooden countertops are avail-able through *some* building supply centers — you'll have to call around to find a distributor near you.

When you have gathered all the stock, cut the parts to the sizes shown, except the door and drawer parts. Cut these later, after you've made the cabinet case.

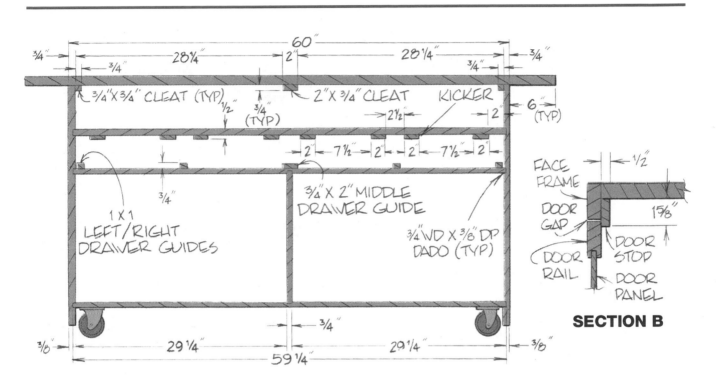

SECTION A

SECTION B

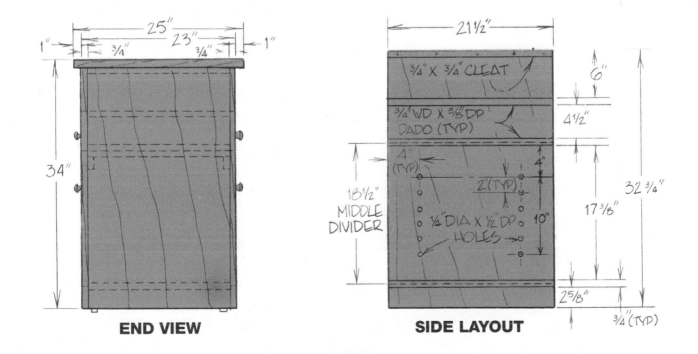

END VIEW

SIDE LAYOUT

3 Cut the dadoes in the sides and shelves.

The plywood parts of the case are assembled with ³/₄″-wide, ³/₈″-deep dadoes. Lay out the dadoes of the sides, middle shelf, and bottom shelf, as shown in the *Side Layout* and *Section A*. Cut the dadoes with a dado cutter or router.

---

4 Drill the holes in the sides, dividers, and cleats.

Drill the holes needed:

- ¹/₄″-diameter, ¹/₂″-deep holes in the sides to hold adjustable shelving supports, as shown in the *Side Layout*
- ³/₁₆″-diameter holes, countersunk, in the middle cleat to attach it to the top, as shown in the *Top View*
- ³/₁₆″-diameter holes, countersunk, in the left and right cleats to attach them to the top and sides

You must drill holes through *both* the edges and the faces of the left and right cleats. These holes will be perpendicular to each other, but they should not cross — you don't drill one hole sideways through another. The spacing of the holes in the cleats is not critical, but it should be fairly even.

---

5 Assemble the face frame.

As shown in the drawings, the face frame members are assembled with wooden plates or "biscuits." Use two plates in each joint for added strength. Cut slots for #00 plates to join parts that are under 2″ wide (such as the top face frame rails and mullions) and #20 plates for those parts 2″ wide and wider. Finish sand the face frame members, then join the parts with glue and plates.

After the glue dries, sand the joints clean and flush. Where you've joined the mullions to the rails, the plates stick out on either side. File these plates flush with the edges of the face frame members. (See Figure 1.)

Note: If you don't have a plate joiner, you can also use dowels and a doweling jig to join the face frame members.

1/Even the smallest (#00) biscuits are too large for some narrow face frame members. After you cut the slots and assemble the frame, the biscuits will stick out on either side of these parts. File the visible biscuits flush with the edges of the members. When you install the doors and drawers, they'll be hidden completely.

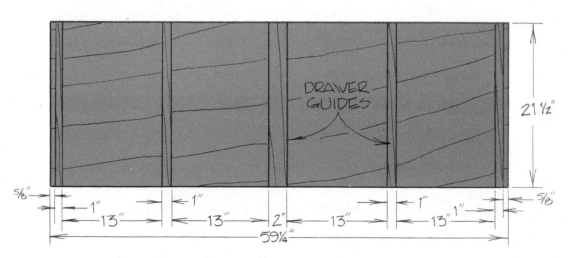

MIDDLE SHELF LAYOUT

6 **Assemble the plywood parts of the cabinet.** Glue the sides, shelves, and divider together, reinforcing the joints with flathead screws. Assemble the parts in this order:

- Fasten the sides to the top shelf.
- Fasten the middle shelf to the divider.
- Slide the middle shelf in place, and fasten it to the sides.
- Slide the bottom shelf in place, and fasten it to the sides and divider.

Countersink the screws that hold the shelves to the divider, so the heads are flush with the surface of the

SHELF-TO-SIDE JOINERY DETAIL

plywood. Drive the screws that hold the shelves to the sides at a steep angle, through the shelves and into the sides, as shown in the *Shelf-to-Side Joinery Detail*. This will keep the screws from showing on the outside of the cabinet.

7 **Assemble the remaining parts of the cabinet.** Fasten the face frame to the cabinet with glue and screws. Counterbore *and* countersink the screws, then hide the heads with wooden plugs. When the glue dries, sand all joints clean and flush. Sand the plugs flush with the surface of the face frame.

Glue the kickers, door stops, and drawer guides in place. Carefully align the drawer guides with the face frame members — the edges of these parts must be flush.

Attach the cleats to the sides and middle face frame stiles with glue and screws. Counterbore and countersink the screws that hold the middle cleat, then cover the heads with wooden plugs. Sand the plugs flush with the surface of the stiles.

Attach the top to the cabinet, driving screws up through the cleats and into the bottom surface of the top.

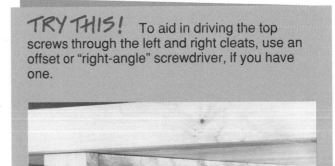

TRY THIS! To aid in driving the top screws through the left and right cleats, use an offset or "right-angle" screwdriver, if you have one.

8 **Cut the door parts.** Measure the dimensions of the door openings in the cabinet. If these measurements have changed from those shown in the drawings, make the necessary changes in the dimensions of the door parts. Cut the door parts to size.

TRY THIS! Many craftsmen prefer to build the doors slightly oversize, then plane and sand them to fit.

9 **Cut the door joinery.** The doors are assembled with haunched mortises and tenons. Make the joints in this order:

- $3/8''$-wide, $3/8''$-deep rabbets in the adjoining edges of the inside door stiles, as shown in *Section C*, so the doors will lap each other
- $1/4''$-wide, $3/8''$-deep grooves in the inside edges of all door stiles and rails

- $1/4''$-wide, $1''$-deep, $1 1/4''$-long mortises in the stiles, $3/8''$ from either end, as shown in the *Door Joinery Detail*
- $1/4''$-thick, $1''$-long tenons on the ends of the rails

Using a band saw or a dovetail saw, notch each tenon to create a haunch. Fit the tenons to their mortises.

10

Assemble and mount the doors. Finish sand the door parts. Assemble the rails and stiles with glue, inserting the tenons in the mortises. Remember that the rabbets on the left and right inside door stiles must face in *opposite* directions, as shown in *Section C*. As you assemble the doors, slide the panels in place but do *not* glue them. Let them float in their grooves. Sand all joints clean and flush, then attach door pulls to the inside stiles.

Mortise the door frames and face frames for butt hinges, then mount the doors on the cabinet so the rabbets in the right inside door stiles lap over those on the left. Install door pulls on the outside of the doors and catches inside the cabinet.

11

Cut the drawer parts. Measure the drawer openings and note any deviation from the plans. Make the necessary changes in the dimensions, then cut the parts to size. As with the doors, you may wish to cut these parts so the assembled drawers will be about 1/16″ wider and taller than the openings. This will allow you to sand each drawer to size, custom fitting it to its opening.

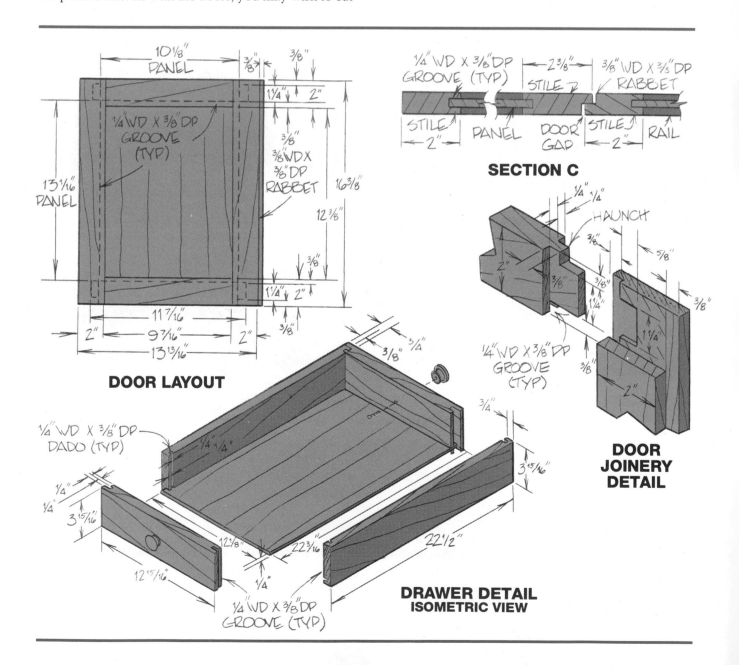

DOOR LAYOUT

SECTION C

DOOR JOINERY DETAIL

DRAWER DETAIL
ISOMETRIC VIEW

12

Cut the drawer joinery. The sides of each drawer are joined to the ends with lock joints (sometimes called dado-and-tongue joints). You can make these joints on a table saw with a dado cutter accessory, as shown in Figures 2, 3, and 4. After making the lock joints, cut ¼"-wide, ⅜"-deep grooves in the inside surface of the sides and ends to hold the bottom. Each groove must be ¼" from the bottom edge.

2/To make a lock joint to join ¾"-thick stock, first cut ¼"-wide, ⅜"-deep dadoes on the inside faces of the drawer sides. Each dado must be ¼" from the end of the board.

3/Adjust the height of the cutter and cut a ¼"-wide, ¾"-deep groove in the ends of the drawer ends. This will create two ¼"-wide, ¾" long tenons on each end.

4/Switch to an ordinary combination saw blade, then trim the **inside** tenons on the drawer ends to ⅜" long. The short tenons should fit the dadoes in the drawer sides.

13

Assemble and fit the drawers.
Assemble the drawers with glue, wiping away the excess. As you put the sides and ends together, slide the bottoms in place but do *not* glue them. Let them float in the grooves. After the glue dries, sand the joints clean and flush. Install drawer pulls, then fit each drawer to its opening, planing, scraping, and sanding away the stock until the drawer operates smoothly.

TRY THIS! Wood expands and contracts with changes in temperature and humidity. You should fit the drawers snugly if you make them in the summer, when it's hot and humid, because the wood will have expanded. Allow a gap of just ¹⁄₆₄" to ¹⁄₃₂" on all sides. When the wood shrinks in the winter, the drawers will still operate smoothly. If you make the drawers in the winter, fit the drawers with a little play — a gap of about ¹⁄₁₆" all around — to allow the wood room to expand when summer comes. If you make the drawers in spring or fall, split the difference — allow a gap of ¹⁄₃₂" to ¹⁄₁₆".

14

Finish the work island. Remove the doors, drawers, and all hardware from the cabinet. Apply a finish to the wooden parts. Coat all sides of the cabinet, inside and out, top and bottom. Apply several coats of wax to the top to keep glue from sticking to the surface. Finally, replace the doors, drawers, and hardware.

Shopmade Retractable Casters

There are two traditional ways to make stationary power tools mobile — mount them on either *retractable* casters or *brake* casters. Unfortunately, commercial retractable casters — casters that can be raised or lowered — are very expensive. Most cost over $100 for a set of four! Brake casters, with a locking brake, swivel even when the brakes are locked, so the tool may move slightly while being used. For these reasons, many craftsmen prefer an immobile tool that sits on four sturdy legs.

These shopmade retractable casters offer an inexpensive, stable alternative. They're extremely easy to make. Simply mount ordinary swivel casters to a 2 x 4. Hinge the 2 x 4 to the tool legs or cabinet so when the 2 x 4 is folded down, the casters lift the tool about 1″. When it's folded up, the tool rests solidly on the floor.

Make a pivoting brace to hold the 2 x 4 in the down position, as shown in the *Pivoting Brace Layout*. Lay out the shape of the brace, then cut it with a band saw or saber saw. Sand the sawed edges and round over the bottom end.

Attach the brace to the tool above the casters with a ³⁄₈″ lag screw and flat washer. (For long 2 x 4s with several casters, you may need several braces — one above each caster.) Also attach hooks and eyes to hold the 2 x 4 in the up position.

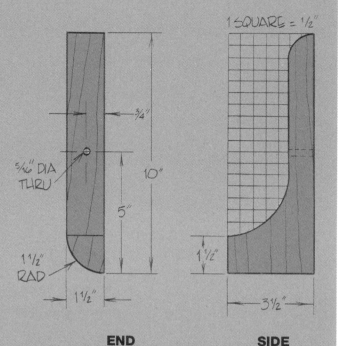

END VIEW   SIDE PATTERN

PIVOTING BRACE LAYOUT

To raise the tool onto the casters and make it mobile, fold the 2 x 4 and casters down. Turn the pivoting brace so it's vertical, pushing the 2 x 4 down. The tool should rise about 1″ off the floor.

To retract the casters, turn the brace so it's horizontal. Fold up the 2 x 4, and the tool will settle back on its legs.

Quick Cabinets

Built-in countertop cabinets can be extremely useful in a workshop. They provide a broad surface on which to work, with drawers and shelves underneath to store both large and small items.

Because they attach to the shop building, they're extremely sturdy. What more could you ask of a piece of shop furniture?

These cabinets are often difficult and expensive to make. Like most built-ins, they normally require a lot of materials, hardware, and time. The cabinets shown, however, are an exception. You can make them from inexpensive materials — hardboard, construction plywood, and pine shelving. They don't require much hardware and they aren't difficult to make or install. With a single exception, you assemble them with butt joints and nail them together.

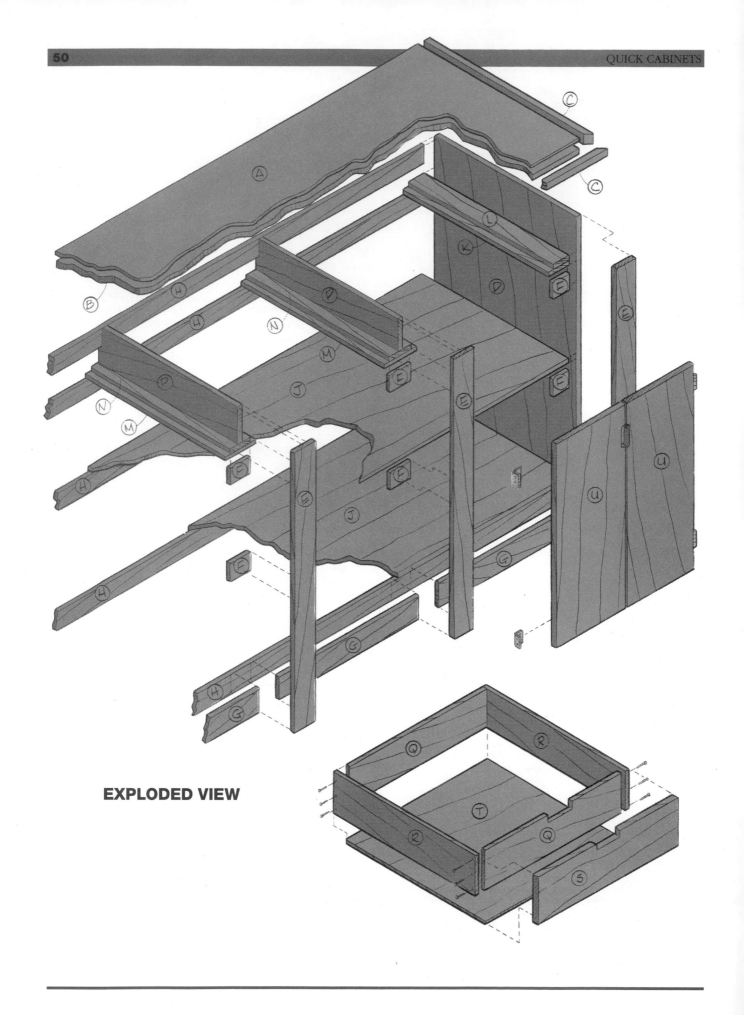

EXPLODED VIEW

Materials List

FINISHED DIMENSIONS

PARTS

A. Counter surface* $\frac{1}{4}''$ x $23\frac{1}{4}''$ x (variable)

B. Countertop** $\frac{3}{4}''$ x $23\frac{1}{4}''$ x (variable)

C. Counter trim $\frac{3}{4}''$ x $1''$ x (variable)

D. Sides** (0–2) $\frac{3}{4}''$ x $21\frac{3}{4}''$ x $35''$

E. Stiles (2 or more) $\frac{3}{4}''$ x $3''$ x $35''$

F. Cleats (4 or more) $\frac{3}{4}''$ x $2\frac{1}{4}''$ x $3''$

G. Toeboards (1 or more) $\frac{3}{4}''$ x $3''$ x $21''$

H. Front/back rails (5) $\frac{3}{4}''$ x $2\frac{1}{4}''$ x (variable)

J. Top/bottom shelves** (2) $\frac{3}{4}''$ x $21\frac{3}{4}''$ x (variable)

K. Left/right drawer supports (2) $\frac{3}{4}''$ x $3''$ x $21\frac{3}{4}''$

L. Left/right drawer guides (2) $\frac{3}{4}''$ x $2\frac{1}{4}''$ x $21\frac{3}{4}''$

M. Middle drawer supports (as needed) $\frac{3}{4}''$ x $4\frac{1}{2}''$ x $21\frac{3}{4}''$

N. Middle drawer guides (as needed) $\frac{3}{4}''$ x $3''$ x $21\frac{3}{4}''$

P. Top braces (1 per middle drawer guide) $\frac{3}{4}''$ x $4\frac{1}{2}''$ x $21\frac{3}{4}''$

Q. Drawer fronts/backs (2 or more) $\frac{1}{2}''$ x $4\frac{7}{8}''$ x $19\frac{7}{8}''$

R. Drawer sides (2 or more) $\frac{1}{2}''$ x $4\frac{7}{8}''$ x $20\frac{7}{8}''$

S. Drawer faces (1 or more) $\frac{3}{4}''$ x $5\frac{7}{8}''$ x $20\frac{7}{8}''$

T. Drawer bottoms (1 or more) $\frac{1}{4}''$ x $20\frac{7}{8}''$ x $20\frac{7}{8}''$

U. Doors (2 or more) $\frac{3}{4}''$ x $10\frac{7}{16}''$ x $25\frac{7}{8}''$

*Make this from tempered hardboard.
**Make these from plywood.

HARDWARE

$\frac{1}{4}''$ x $3\frac{1}{2}''$ Lag screws (8 or more)
$\frac{1}{4}''$ Flat washers (8 or more)
4d Finishing nails ($\frac{1}{4}$ lb. or more)
6d Finishing nails ($\frac{1}{4}$ lb. or more)
$\frac{7}{8}''$ Wire brads (1 box or more)
Wraparound hinges and mounting screws (4 or more)
Door catches (2 or more)

---

1 Determine how wide to make the cabinet. Measure the space where you wish to install the cabinet, and decide how wide to make it. As drawn, the cabinet is made up of two similar modules — an *end* unit (two stiles) and a *middle* unit (one stile — it shares the second stile with the unit next to it). The first end unit is 27″ wide, and each additional unit adds another 24″ to the width of the installed cabinet. Adjust the cabinet width to fit your space by adding and subtracting units, or by adjusting the width of each unit. It's best to keep all the units the same width, however, so that the parts can be easily mass-produced.

---

2 Select the stock and cut the parts to size. Once you know the width of the cabinet (and the width of the individual units), calculate the parts you need and their dimensions. From this, figure the amount of lumber and plywood needed. For each unit as drawn, you can figure *approximately* 10 board feet of one-by ($\frac{3}{4}''$ thick) stock, a 4′ x 4′ sheet of $\frac{3}{4}''$ plywood, a 2′ x 2′ sheet of $\frac{1}{4}''$ plywood, and a 2′ x 2′ sheet of tempered hardboard. Add an additional 4′ x 4′ sheet of $\frac{3}{4}''$ plywood to make the sides for the end units.

You can build this project from almost any sort of wood or sheet materials, depending on the look you want and what you can afford. The cabinets shown are made from shelving (#2 pine) and A-C construction-grade plywood. You can also use cabinet-grade materials if you don't mind the expense. Or, if you want to save money, use particleboard or hardboard.

Once you've purchased the materials, cut them to the sizes needed, except the doors and drawer parts. Cut these later, after you've installed the cabinet case.

Note: If you can, cut the front rail so that it runs the entire length of the cabinet without a break. If you can't do this, plan the break so that it will be behind a toeboard on the assembled cabinet, not behind a stile.

3

Cut notches in the top braces. The one and only joint (other than butt joints) in this entire project is a single notch in the back end of each top brace, as shown in the *Top Brace Layout*. This notch fits around the top back rail. Cut this with a saber saw or a hand saw.

4

Attach the back rails to the wall. There is no back to the cabinet; instead, the back rails are attached directly to the wall, as shown in the *Back Rail Layout*. Locate the studs in the wall, then mark the positions of the rails on the wall with a snap line. Secure the rails to the wall studs with lag screws and flat washers.

Note: If you're attaching the rails to a masonry wall, first drill the wall with a masonry bit and install expansive shields in the holes. Drive the lag screws through the rails and into the shields. (See Figure 1.)

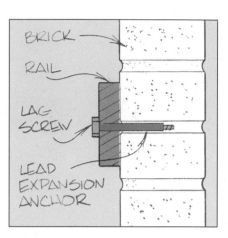

1/Use expansive anchors to attach the rails to a masonry wall. These anchors expand, wedging themselves in the wall, when you drive lag screws into them.

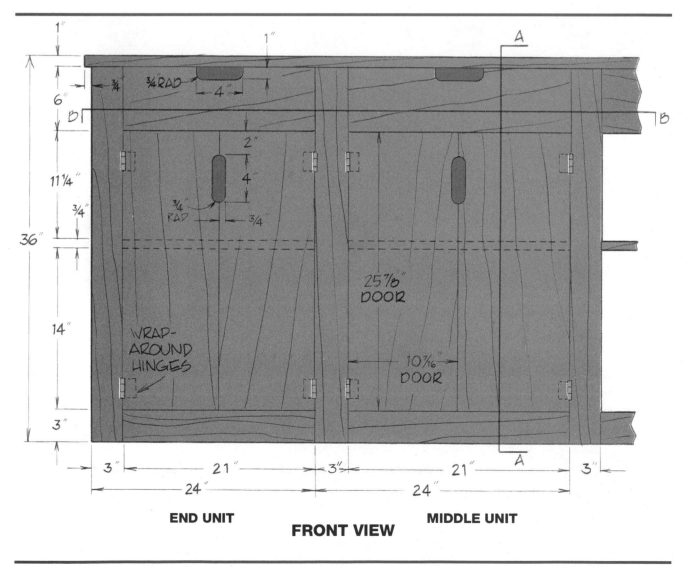

END UNIT   **MIDDLE UNIT**

FRONT VIEW

5

Assemble the stiles, toeboards, front rail, and cleats. Finish sand all the outside surfaces of the cabinet parts. Measure the positions of the cleats on the front rails, as shown in the *Stile Layout,* then attach them with glue and finishing nails. Lay out the stiles and toeboards on the floor of your shop with the back surfaces facing up. Use a framing square to make sure the toeboards are square to the stiles. Glue and nail the front rail to the toeboards and stiles, tying all the parts together, as shown in the *Face Frame Assembly Detail.* This will make a face frame.

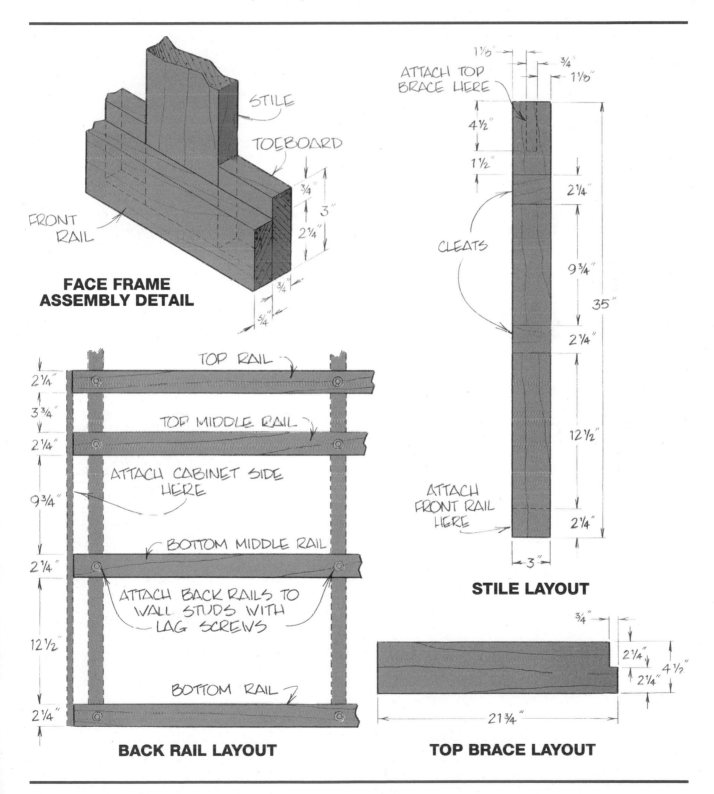

FACE FRAME ASSEMBLY DETAIL

STILE

TOEBOARD

FRONT RAIL

STILE LAYOUT

ATTACH TOP BRACE HERE

CLEATS

ATTACH FRONT RAIL HERE

BACK RAIL LAYOUT

TOP RAIL

TOP MIDDLE RAIL

ATTACH CABINET SIDE HERE

BOTTOM MIDDLE RAIL

ATTACH BACK RAILS TO WALL STUDS WITH LAG SCREWS

BOTTOM RAIL

TOP BRACE LAYOUT

6 **Install the cabinet ends and face frame assembly.** Nail the cabinet ends to the ends of the back rails with finishing nails. Then attach the face frame assembly to the cabinet ends with glue and nails. Set the heads of the nails.

7 **Attach the shelves.** With a helper, drop the bottom shelf in place so it rests on the front rail and bottom back rail. If the parts aren't perfectly square to each other, you may have to shift the cabinet ends and the face frame slightly to seat the shelf properly. When the shelf is in place, nail it to the rails and set the heads of the nails.

Repeat for the top shelf, resting it on the cleats and the bottom middle back rail. Check the spacing between the stiles, making sure the door openings are all even and that the stiles are plumb. Also make sure the stiles are square to the toeboards. Then nail the top shelf in place and set the nail heads.

8 **Install the drawer supports, drawer guides, and top braces.** Attach the top braces to the middle drawer guides with glue and nails. Then attach the drawer guides to the drawer supports, as shown in the *Left/Right Drawer Support Assembly Detail* and *Middle Drawer Support Assembly Detail*.

Place these assemblies so the drawer support rests on the top middle rail and the top cleat as shown in *Section A*. The notched end of the brace should fit between the top rail and the top middle rail (just below it). Check the spacing between the supports, and be sure they are perfectly parallel. The middle supports must protrude ³⁄₄″ on either side of the stiles. The top edge of the top braces must be flush with the top edge of the top rail and the top ends of the stiles. When you're satisfied the parts are properly positioned, nail them in place. Set the heads of the nails.

9 **Install the countertop, countertop surface, and trim.** Place the countertop so it rests on the back rail, top braces, sides, and stiles. Check that the parts are square to each other, then nail the countertop in place. Cover the countertop with ¼″ hardboard. Don't glue the hardboard in place, just tack it down with brads. This will allow you to easily replace the hardboard when the countertop surface becomes stained, discolored, or beat-up.

Trim the countertop and countertop surface with ³⁄₄″-thick, 1″-wide stock to hide the edges. Miter the adjoining corners of the trim, then nail the trim in place. Set the heads of the nails. Don't glue the trim to the countertop, so you can easily remove it when you want to replace the surface.

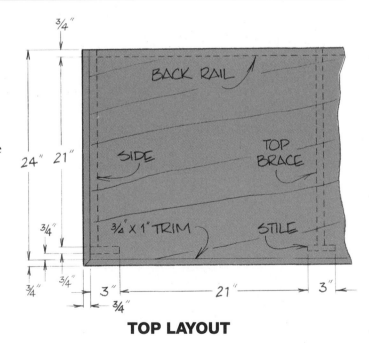

TOP LAYOUT

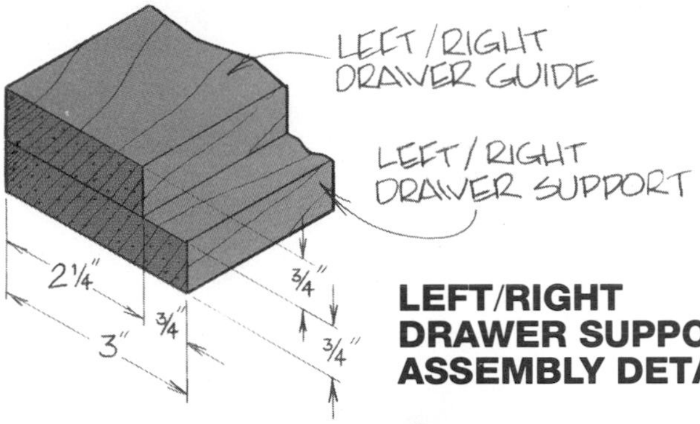
LEFT/RIGHT DRAWER GUIDE
LEFT/RIGHT DRAWER SUPPORT
2¼″
3″
¾″
¾″
¾″

LEFT/RIGHT DRAWER SUPPORT ASSEMBLY DETAIL

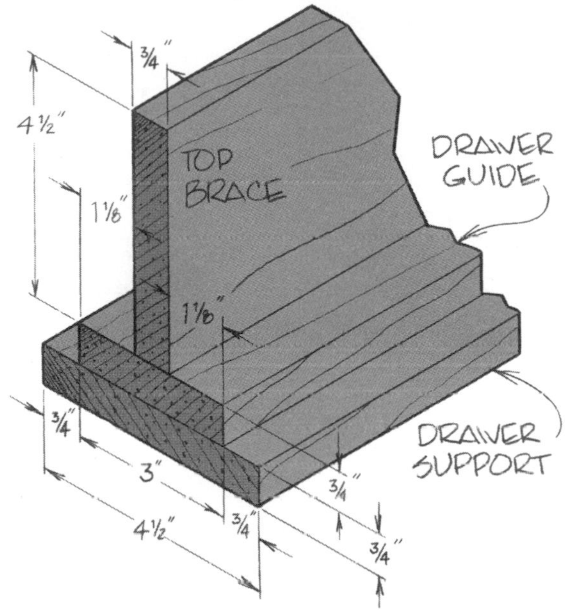
TOP BRACE
DRAWER GUIDE
DRAWER SUPPORT
4½″
1⅛″
1⅛″
¾″
¾″
3″
4½″
¾″
¾″
¾″

MIDDLE DRAWER SUPPORT ASSEMBLY DETAIL

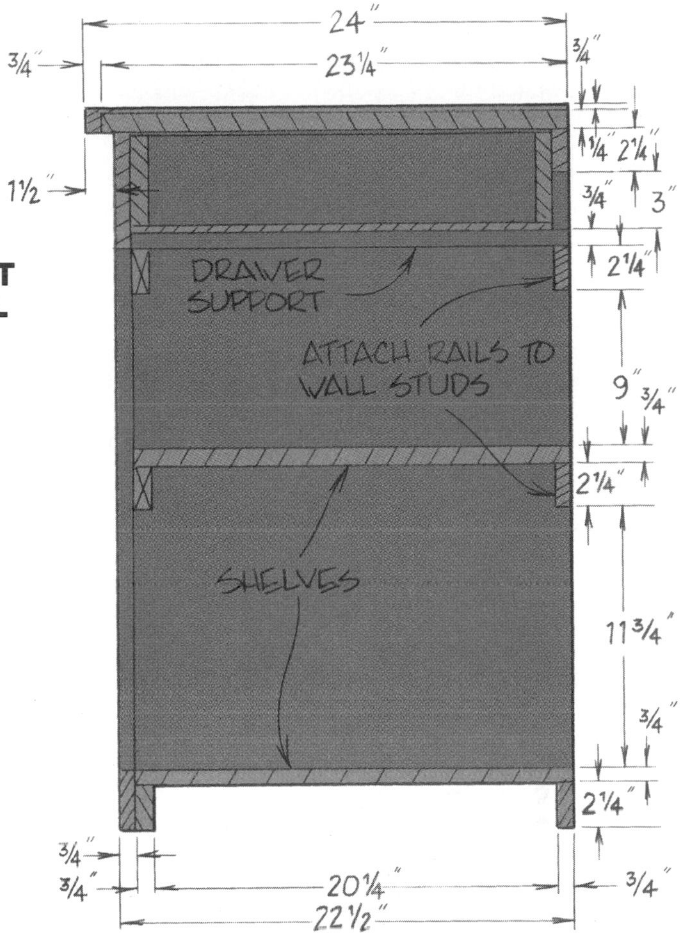
24″
23¼″
¾″
¾″
1½″
¼″
2¼″
¾″
3″
2¼″
DRAWER SUPPORT
ATTACH RAILS TO WALL STUDS
9″
¾″
2¼″
SHELVES
11¾″
¾″
2¼″
¾″
¾″
20¼″
22½″
¾″

SECTION A

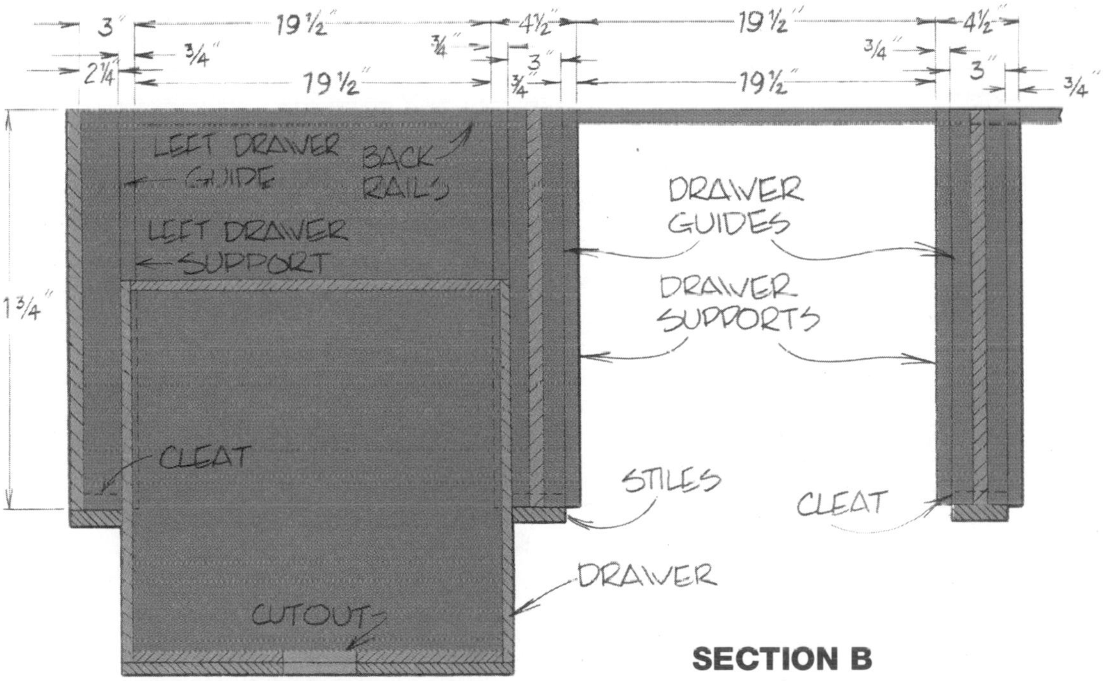
3″
19½″
4½″
19½″
4½″
¾″
2¼″
¾″
19½″
¾″
3″
¾″
19½″
¾″
3″
¾″
21¾″
LEFT DRAWER GUIDE
BACK RAILS
LEFT DRAWER SUPPORT
DRAWER GUIDES
DRAWER SUPPORTS
CLEAT
STILES
CLEAT
DRAWER
CUTOUT

SECTION B

10

Build and install the drawers. Glue and nail the drawer fronts, backs, sides, and bottoms together, and set the nails. Sand the joints clean and flush, then glue the faces on the drawer fronts.

Lay out the cutout in the top edge of each drawer face, as shown in the *Front View*. Cut through the face and drawer front with a saber saw or coping saw, then sand the sawed edges.

Slide the drawer into place and test the sliding action. If a drawer binds, sand or plane some stock from the drawer sides until it works smoothly.

11

Cut and install the doors. Lay out the cutouts in the inside edges of the doors, as shown in the *Front View*. Cut these with a saber saw or coping saw and sand the sawed edges.

Mount the doors to the cabinet stiles with *wraparound* hinges. (See Figure 2.) Don't use ordinary butt hinges or piano hinges — the screws will not hold tight if you drive them into the edge of the plywood doors. Wraparound hinges allow you to drive the screws through the back face of the plywood.

2/Use wraparound hinges to mount the doors to the cabinet. Ordinary hinges may tear loose from the plywood edges.

12

Finish the cabinet. Remove the doors, drawers, and all the hinges from the cabinet. Do any necessary touch-up sanding, then apply a finish or paint to the cabinet, doors, and drawer fronts. Apply several coats of wax to the countertop surface — this will keep glue from sticking to it. Finally, replace the drawers, doors, and hinges.

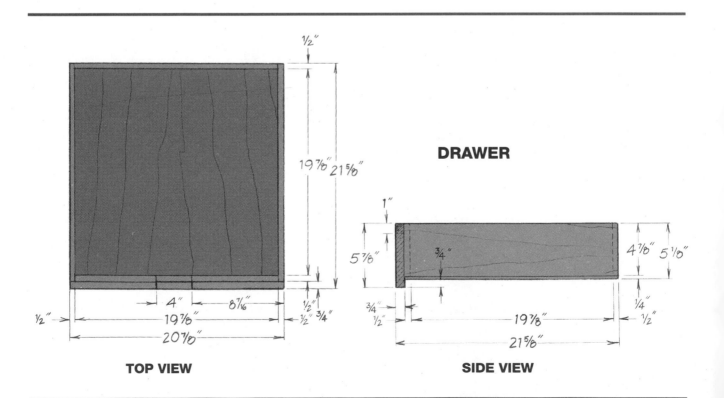

TOP VIEW

DRAWER

SIDE VIEW

Clamp Racks

Typically, woodworkers spend the first half of their careers acquiring enough clamps to meet every possible clamping contingency, and the second half wondering where to put all their clamps. Novice woodworkers never have enough clamps; veterans never have enough clamp racks. For those of you who have crossed this line, here are three easy-to-build clamp storage devices.

These simple *peg rails* were built by Judy Ditmer, a professional turner in Tipp City, Ohio. They are designed to hold long clamps, such as bar clamps and pipe clamps. Simply slip the head of the clamp between the pegs.

The *hand screw holders* are another of Judy Ditmer's designs. The handles on the hand screws rest in the scalloped arms of each holder. The advantage of this particular holder is that you don't have to adjust the screw to place it in the rack. The arms will support a hand screw with the jaws wide open, closed tight, or anywhere in between.

The *pipe clamp caddy* holds and organizes pipe clamps of all sizes *and* brings them to the job. Slide the pipes into the holes in the rails, and then roll the caddy wherever it's needed. This was designed by Larry Callahan of West Milton, Ohio.

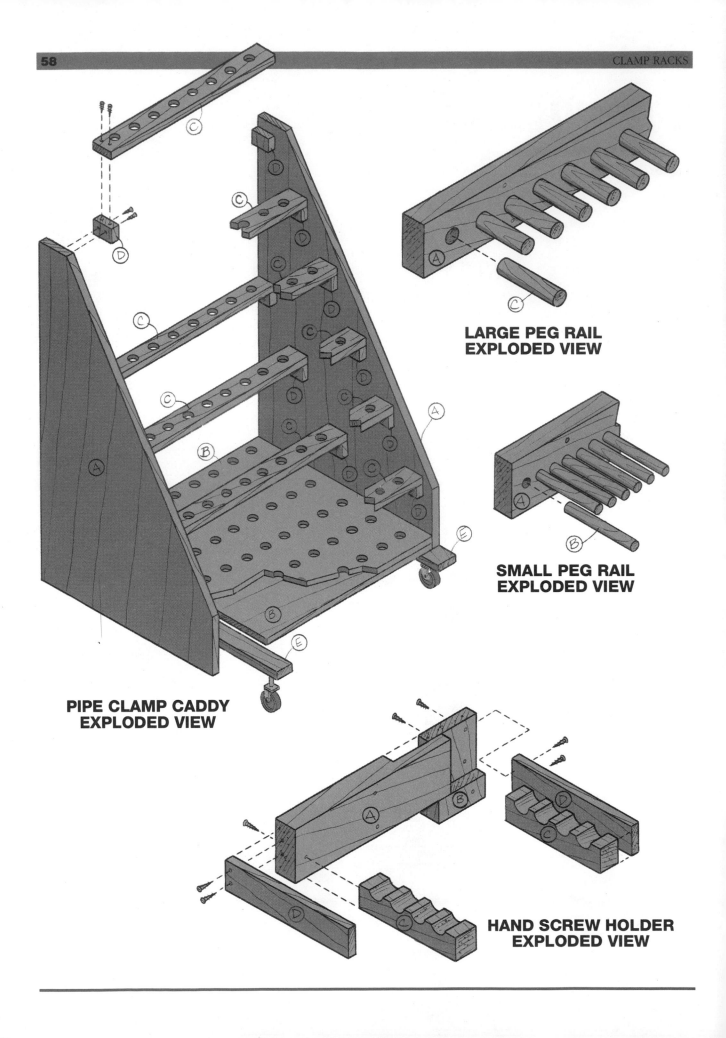

LARGE PEG RAIL EXPLODED VIEW

SMALL PEG RAIL EXPLODED VIEW

PIPE CLAMP CADDY EXPLODED VIEW

HAND SCREW HOLDER EXPLODED VIEW

Materials List

FINISHED DIMENSIONS

PARTS

Peg Rails

A. Rail   1½" x 3½" x (variable)

B. Small pegs (variable)   ⅝" dia. x 5"

C. Large pegs (variable)   1" dia. x 4¼"

Hand Screw Holder

A. Back   1½" x 3½" x (variable)

B. Leg   1½" x 3½" x (variable)

C. Arms (2)   1½" x 1½" x (variable)

D. Arm supports (2)   ½" x 2" x (variable)

Pipe Clamp Caddy

A. Sides* (2)   ¾" x 22¼" x 37½"

B. Bases* (2)   ¾" x 21½" x 22¼"

C. Racks (9)   ¾" x 2¼" x 21½"

D. Cleats (18)   ¾" x 1½" x 2¼"

E. Mounts (2)   ¾" x 2¼" x 26¾"

*Make these from plywood.

HARDWARE

Peg Rails

¼" x 4" Lag screws (2–4)

¼" Flat washers (2–4)

Hand Screw Holder

#10 x 1½" Flathead wood screws (6)

#12 x 2½" Flathead wood screws (2)

¼" x 4" Lag screws (2)

¼" Flat washers (2)

Pipe Clamp Caddy

1¼" Drywall screws (96–102)

2" Swivel casters and mounting screws (4)

Making the Peg Rails

1. Determine the size and length of each peg rail.

Take an inventory of your long clamps to determine the types and number of each that you want to hang. Use the small rail to hang sliding C-clamps and clamps with narrow bars. Use the large rail to hang pipe clamps and clamps with wide bars.

Calculate the length of each rail and the number of pegs you need. You can make the rails any length and use any number of pegs, depending on how many clamps (and how much wall space) you have. You may also have to adjust the spacing of the pegs for the clamps.

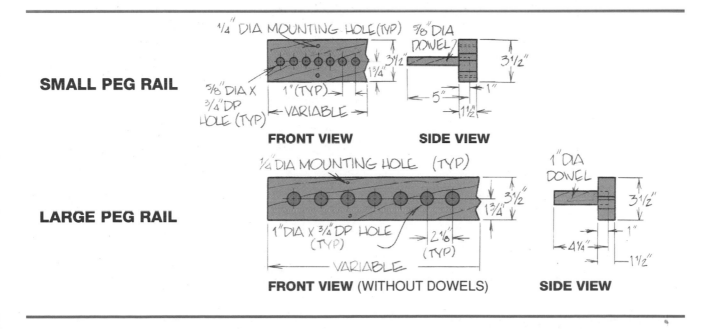

SMALL PEG RAIL   FRONT VIEW   SIDE VIEW

LARGE PEG RAIL   FRONT VIEW (WITHOUT DOWELS)   SIDE VIEW

2

Select the stock and cut the parts to size. The rails can be made from 2 x 4s, and the pegs from ordinary dowel stock. Purchase clear, kiln-dried 2 x 4s. Construction-grade wood is not thoroughly dried and, in time, it may warp or twist.

When you have gathered the materials, cut them to the sizes needed.

3

Drill holes in the rails. The pegs are held in stopped holes in the rails. Drill these holes at least 1″ deep, as shown in the *Small Peg Rail/Side View* and *Large Peg Rail/Side View*. The deep holes help to support the load on the pegs.

4

Assemble and mount the peg rails. Locate the studs in the wall where you want to hang each peg rail. Mark each rail where it will cross the studs, and drill ¼″-diameter mounting holes at these marks. Sand the rails, then glue the pegs in the rails. When the glue dries, mount the rails to the wall, driving lag screws with flat washers through the mounting holes and into the wall studs.

Making the Hand Screw Holders

1

Determine the size of the holders. The size of each hand screw holder — and the lengths of its various parts — depends on the size of the hand screws that it must hold. Take an inventory of your hand screws, sorting them according to size. Then measure each size, recording the combined length of the screw measured from handle to handle, the distance between the screws, and the diameter of the handles. These measurements are designated A, B, and C on the *Hand Screw Measurement Detail*.

Determine how many holders you need — each holder will store four hand screws of one size *only*. Then determine the length of the parts and the size of the scallops using these simple formulas:

- Back length = A + ¼″
- Leg length = B + 3½″
- Scallop diameter = C
- Arm length = 4C + 2½″
- Arm support length = 4C + 4″

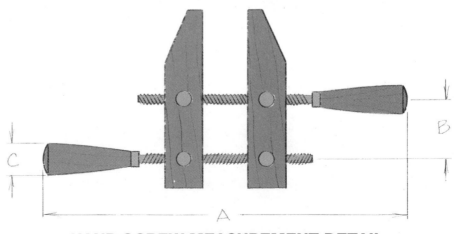

HAND SCREW MEASUREMENT DETAIL

2

Select the stock and cut the parts to size. All the parts can be made from 2 x 4s. Purchase clear, kiln-dried stock — construction-grade wood is not thoroughly dried. In time, it will shrink and the arms may come loose or the hand screws will no longer fit.

When you have purchased the stock, plane the ½″-thick stock needed for the arm supports. Then cut the parts to the sizes needed, except the arms. For the arms, cut a single length of 2 x 4 stock to the correct length, but do not rip it into 2 x 2s yet.

3

Make the scallops and rip the arms to width. Mark a line down the center of the arm stock, along the length. Measure and mark the center of each scallop along this line. Drill a hole through each mark the same diameter as the hand screw handles (measurement C). There should be ½″ between the edges of the holes.

Rip the arm stock in two parts, right down the center. (See Figure 1.) Each part will have four scallops along one edge. Then rip the edges *without* scallops, trimming the arms to 1½″ wide.

1/To make the scallops in the arms, first drill a series of evenly spaced holes down the center of the arm stock. Then rip the stock in two, splitting the holes. **Sawguard removed for clarity.**

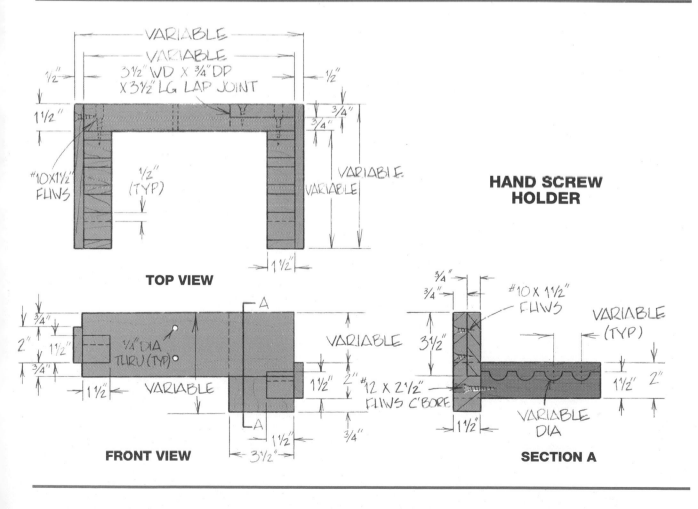

HAND SCREW HOLDER

TOP VIEW

FRONT VIEW

SECTION A

4

Cut the lap joints. The back and the leg are lapped at the adjoining ends, as shown in the *Hand Screw Holder/Top View*. Cut these laps with a dado cutter or combination table saw blade. (See Figures 2 and 3.)

*2/To make a lap joint on a table saw with a combination saw blade, adjust the blade height to precisely half the **thickness** of the boards to be lapped. Cut the cheek of each lap, as shown.*

*3/Readjust the blade height so that it's equal to the **width** of the boards. Mount each board in a tenoning jig to hold it vertically, then cut the face of the lap.*

5

Assemble and mount the holder. Sand the parts smooth, then assemble the holder with glue and screws. Counterbore and/or countersink the screws as shown in the *Hand Screw Holder/Top View*. Sand all joints clean and flush.

Locate the studs in the wall where you want to hang the holders. Mark the backs where they will cross the studs, and drill ¼"-diameter mounting holes at these marks. Mount the holders to the wall, driving lag screws with flat washers through the holes and into the studs.

Making the Pipe Clamp Caddy

1

Determine the size of the caddy. As shown, this caddy will hold 48 pipe clamps. This may be too large or too small for your collection. Take an inventory, then reduce or add to the number of racks on the caddy as needed.

2

Select the stock and cut the parts to size. To make this project as designed, you need about 8 board feet of hardwood and one 4' x 8' sheet of ¾" plywood. The caddy shown is made from birch and construction-grade fir plywood, but you may use any durable stock.

When you have gathered the materials, cut the parts to the sizes needed.

3

Drill the holes in the base and racks. The pipe clamps are held in the caddy by inserting them in holes in the racks and base. These holes are large enough to accommodate ½", ¾", and 1"-diameter pipes.

Drill 1⅛"-diameter holes through the racks. These holes should be evenly spaced, 2½" apart, as shown on the *Pipe Clamp Caddy/Top View*. Then drill a grid of 1⅛"-diameter holes through the base, arranged as shown in the *Base Layout*.

4

Assemble the caddy. Measure and mark the locations of the racks and cleats on the sides, as shown in the *Pipe Clamp Caddy/Section A*. Drill ⅛″-diameter pilot holes in the cleats, then attach the cleats to the sides with glue and screws.

Glue the bases together, then attach the sides to the bases with glue and screws. Drill ⅛″-diameter pilot holes through the ends of the racks, and attach the racks to the cleats with glue and screws. As you drive the screws, check that the rack holes line up with those in the base.

Attach swivel casters to the mounts, near each end. Then attach the mounts to the base and sides with glue and screws.

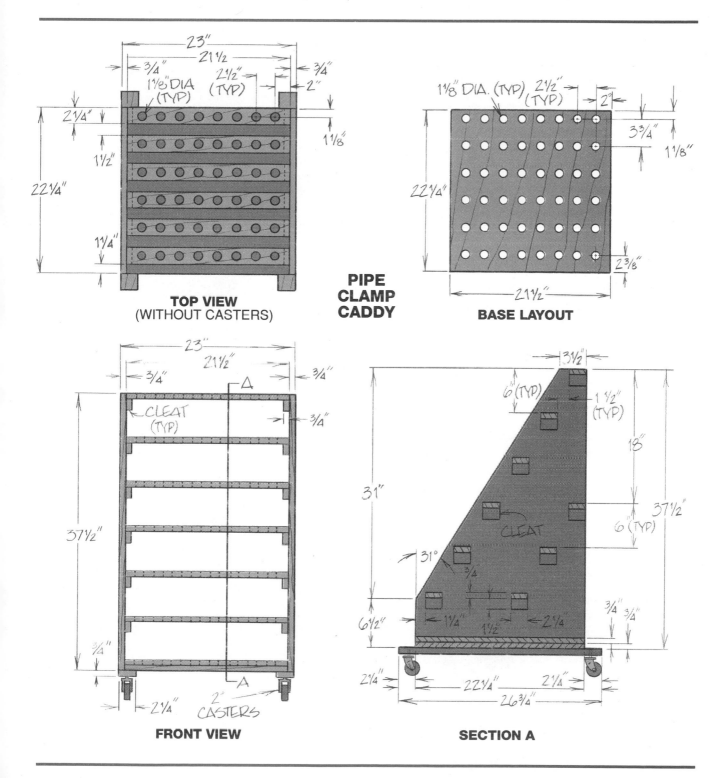

PIPE CLAMP CADDY

TOP VIEW
(WITHOUT CASTERS)

BASE LAYOUT

FRONT VIEW

SECTION A

Knockdown Assembly Table

A s you assemble projects of various sizes, you may find yourself wishing your workbench could be adjusted to various heights to suit them. It's much easier to assemble a large project on a low bench, or a small project on a high bench. That's why furniture manufacturers employ *assembly tables* of different heights for different pieces.

Unfortunately, most home workshops don't have the room for three or four assembly tables. But you may be able to find room for this one. It adjusts to several different heights, from 8¾″ to 34¾″. Furthermore, when not in use, it knocks down and stores flat.

This versatile table is the invention of Judy Ditmer, professional turner and the proprietor of Heartwood (her woodworking shop) in Tipp City, Ohio. To use it, put together pairs of leg assemblies into X-shapes, then stack the Xs to make the table the required height. Finally, rest the top on the legs. All the components fit together with brackets or ⅞″-diameter dowels. ✹

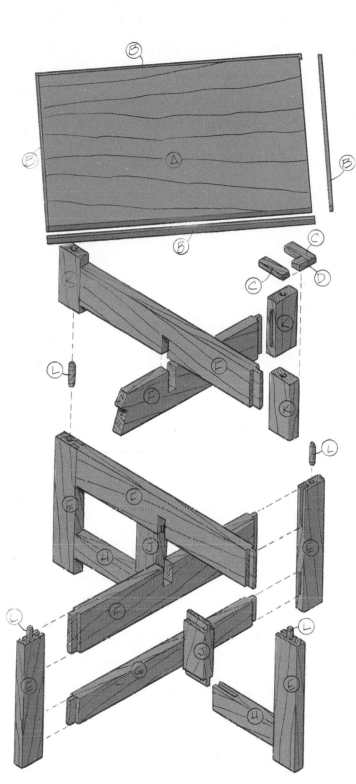

EXPLODED VIEW

Materials List

FINISHED DIMENSIONS

PARTS

Top

A.	Worktable*	3/4″ x 30″ x 30″
B.	Trim (4)	1/4″ x 3/4″ x 30½″
C.	Bracket arms (4)	3/4″ x 1¼″ x 4″
D.	Bracket spacers (2)	3/4″ x 1¼″ x 1⁹/₁₆″

Tall Leg Assemblies (2)

E.	Legs (4)	1½″ x 3½″ x 18″
F.	Rails (2)	1½″ x 5½″ x 31″
G.	Long bottom rail	1½″ x 3½″ x 31″
H.	Short bottom rails (2)	1½″ x 3½″ x 14¾″
J.	Stiles (2)	1½″ x 3½″ x 9″

Short Leg Assemblies (4)

F.	Rails (4)	1½″ x 5½″ x 31″
K.	Legs (8)	1½″ x 3½″ x 8″
L.	Dowels (8)	7/8″ dia. x 2¾″

Make this from plywood.

HARDWARE

4d Finishing nails (48)
1″ Wire brads (24)

1

***Select the stock and cut the parts to
size.*** To build this project, you need two 2 x 6s,
three 2 x 4s, a 4′ x 4′ piece of ³⁄₄″ cabinet-grade plywood, and some scraps of hardwood. If available,
purchase clear, kiln-dried 2 x 4s and 2 x 6s. Ordinary
construction-grade lumber isn't sufficiently dried for
this project. It will shrink and warp as it dries out, and
in a few months the leg assemblies won't fit together
properly.

Once you've purchased the stock, cut all the parts to
the sizes shown in the Materials List, except the trim.
Wait to fit this to the worktable. Chamfer both ends of
the dowels.

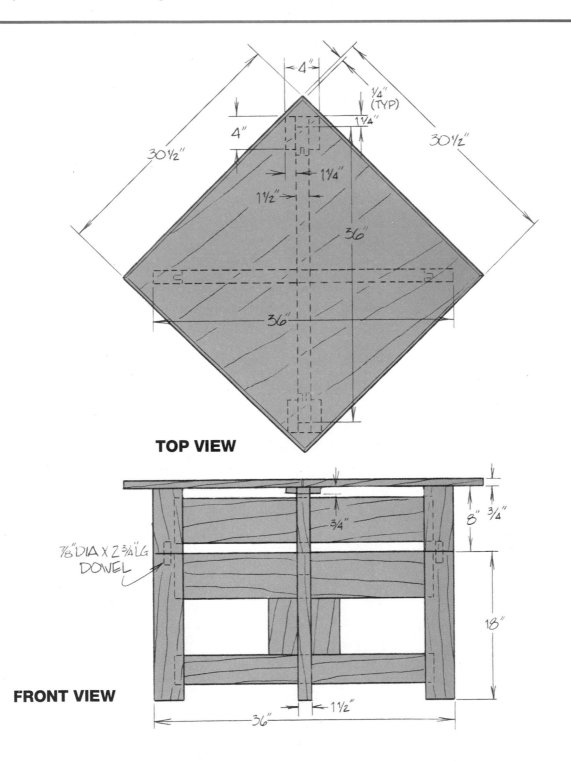

TOP VIEW

FRONT VIEW

2 **Cut the lap joints.** The rails are notched to lap each other, as shown in the *Short Leg Assembly/ Side View, Tall Leg Assembly #1/Side View,* and *Tall Leg Assembly #2/Side View.* To make the 1½″-wide, 2¾″-long notches, first saw the cheeks with a hand saw or table saw. Then knock out the waste with a chisel.

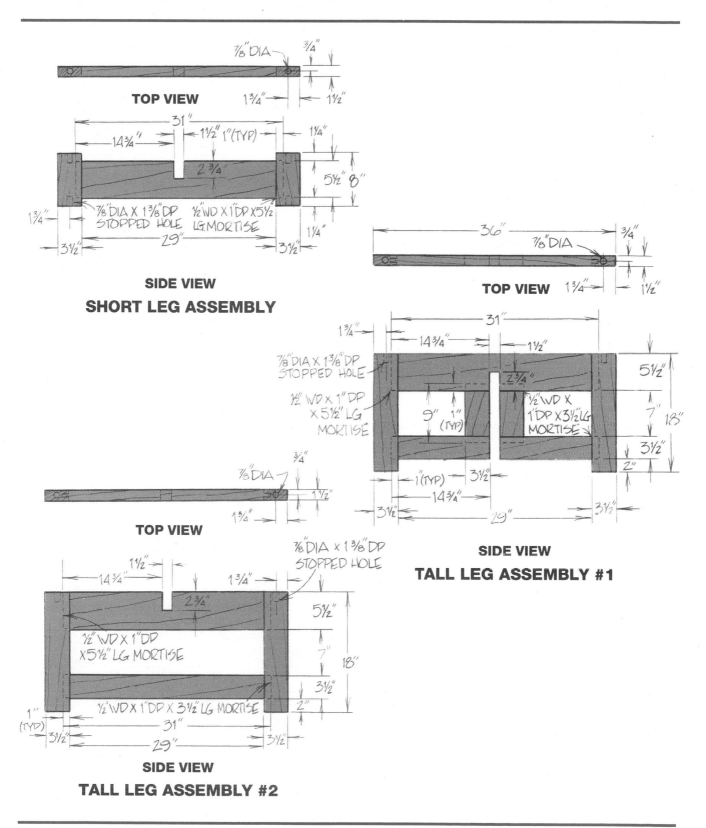

3

Cut the mortises and tenons in the legs, rails, and stiles. The leg assemblies are joined with simple mortises and tenons. (See Figures 1, 2, and 3.)

1/To make the mortises in the legs and rails, first score the edges of the mortises with a marking gauge. Also, make a deep score down the middle of the waste to keep the bit from wandering or deflecting in the soft wood.

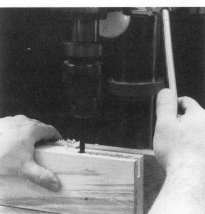

2/Using a brad-point bit or piloted Forstner bit, drill a series of overlapping 1/2"-diameter holes to rough out the mortise. Clean up the sides and square the blind ends of the mortise with a chisel.

Make the following joints:

- 1/2"-wide, 1"-deep, 3½"-long mortises in the #1 top rail, on either side of the notch
- 1/2"-thick, 1"-long tenons on both ends of the rails, long bottom rail, and stiles, and the unmortised end of the short bottom rails
- 1/2"-wide, 1"-deep, 5½"-long mortises in the tall legs, starting at the inside top ends, as shown in the *Tall Leg Assembly #1/Side View* and *Tall Leg Assembly #2/Side View*
- 1/2"-wide, 1"-deep, 5½"-long mortises in the short legs, 1¼" from both ends, as shown in the *Short Leg Assembly/Side View*
- 1/2"-wide, 1"-deep, 3½"-long mortises in the tall legs, 2" from the bottom ends
- 1/2"-wide, 1"-deep, 3½"-long mortises in the short bottom rails, starting at the inside ends

3/Score the cheeks of the tenons with a marking gauge to prevent the soft wood from chipping or tearing out. Cut the tenons on the ends of the rails and stiles with a dado cutter. Use a stop block to gauge the length of each tenon.

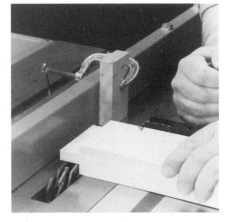

4

Drill dowel holes in the legs. As you stack the leg assemblies on top of each other, dowels align the assemblies and hold them together. To accommodate these dowels, drill 7/8"-diameter, 1 3/8"-deep holes in *both* ends of the short legs, and the *top* ends of the tall legs. These holes must be centered precisely in the ends of the legs. (See Figure 4.)

4/To position the dowel holes in the legs precisely, make a simple doweling jig from hardwood. Clamp each leg securely in the jig before you bore the hole in the end. Attach a stop collar to the bit to stop the drilling at a depth of 1 3/8".

5

Assemble the legs. Finish sand all the parts you've made so far, then glue the leg assemblies together. Do *not* glue the dowels in the holes; leave them loose. Reinforce the tenons in the mortises by driving two or three finishing nails through each joint. When the glue dries, set the nails and sand each joint clean and flush.

6

Assemble the table. Cut the trim, mitering the adjoining ends at 45°. Glue the trim to the edges of the worktable, holding it in place with wire brads. When the glue dries, set the heads of the brads. Sand the trim flush with the worktable surface.

Turn the table over and mark the positions of the brackets. Glue the bracket arms and spacers in place, holding the parts in position with wire brads. When the glue dries, set the heads of the brads.

7

Apply a finish. Do any necessary touch-up sanding to the worktable and leg assemblies. Then apply a finish to the completed project. When the finish dries, wax the top surface of the worktable, building up a protective coat. The wax will help prevent glue from sticking to the table.

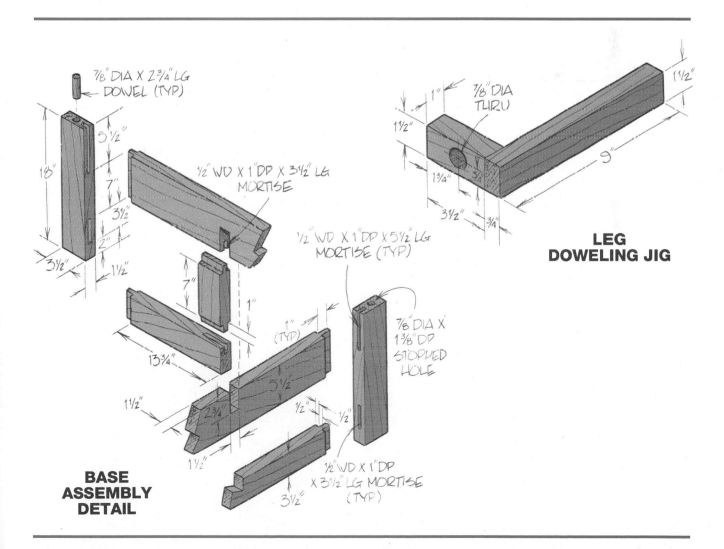

BASE ASSEMBLY DETAIL

LEG DOWELING JIG

Router Mortising Jig

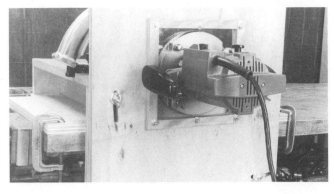

A router table increases the versatility of a router a hundredfold. It holds the router so you can move the work across the bit, which, for most operations, gives you better control. The jig shown further extends the router's possibilities. Like the table, it holds the router so you can concentrate on the work. But instead of keeping the bit vertical, it holds the machine so the bit is *horizontal*.

There are several important advantages to routing horizontally. For example, you can safely and easily make plunge cuts in any surface by moving the stock into the bit. This is awkward to do on a router table — you have to hold the stock above the table and lower it onto the bit. A hand-held plunge router only allows you to cut the face of a board, and you must use special jigs to hold the stock if you want to make a plunge cut in an edge or end. With this router mortising table, however, you simply place the wood on the worktable, adjust the depth of cut, and slowly feed the wood into the bit. This, in turn, simplifies cutting mortises, blind dadoes, and closed-end slots.

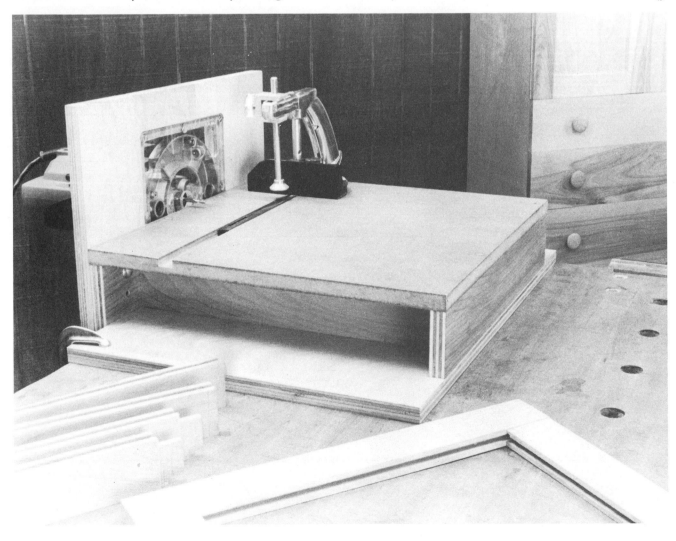

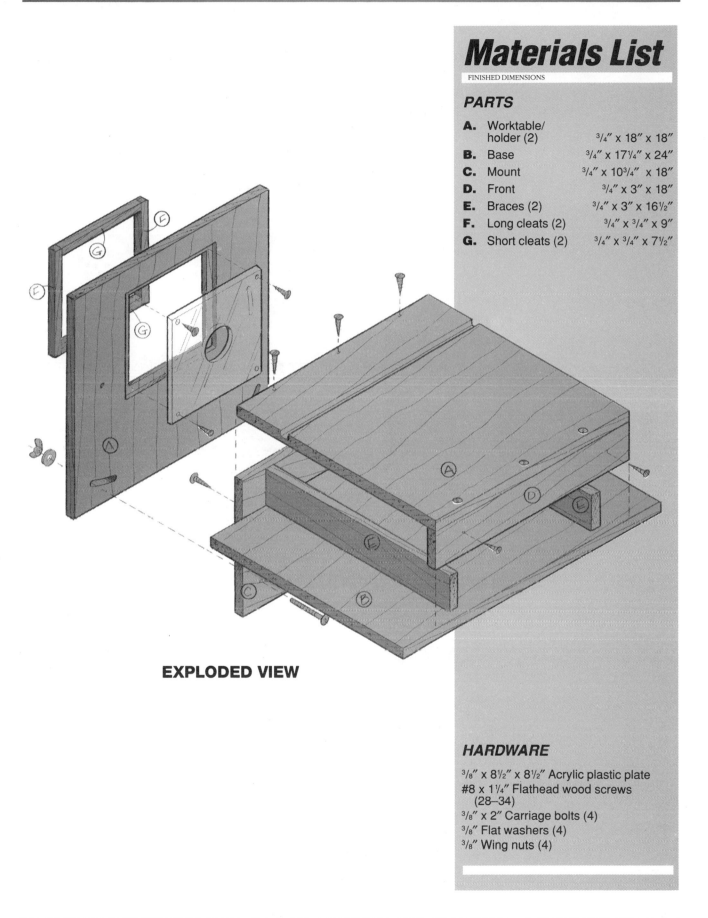

EXPLODED VIEW

Materials List

FINISHED DIMENSIONS

PARTS

A. Worktable/
    holder (2) $3/4''$ x 18" x 18"
B. Base $3/4''$ x 17¼" x 24"
C. Mount $3/4''$ x 10¾" x 18"
D. Front $3/4''$ x 3" x 18"
E. Braces (2) $3/4''$ x 3" x 16½"
F. Long cleats (2) $3/4''$ x $3/4''$ x 9"
G. Short cleats (2) $3/4''$ x $3/4''$ x 7½"

HARDWARE

$3/8''$ x 8½" x 8½" Acrylic plastic plate
#8 x 1¼" Flathead wood screws
   (28–34)
$3/8''$ x 2" Carriage bolts (4)
$3/8''$ Flat washers (4)
$3/8''$ Wing nuts (4)

1

Select the stock and cut the parts to size. To make this project you'll need some scraps of hardwood and a 4′ x 4′ piece of a very flat ¾″-thick material. The mortising table shown is made from Baltic birch plywood, but you may also use MDF board or particleboard with a laminate covering.

When you have gathered the materials, cut them to the sizes shown in the Materials List. Make sure that all the corners are precisely 90°. The accuracy of this project depends on the mount and holder being square to the worktable.

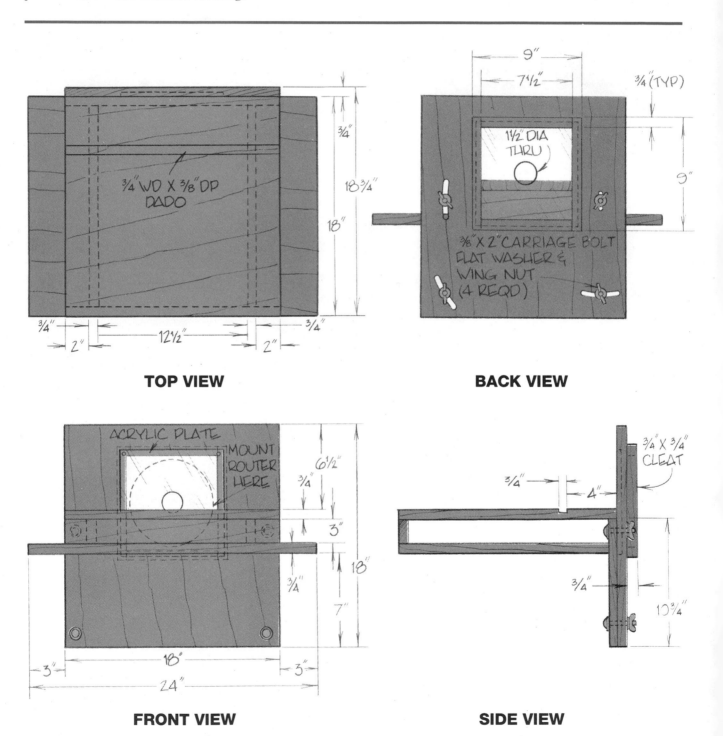

TOP VIEW

BACK VIEW

FRONT VIEW

SIDE VIEW

2

Make the cutout in the holder. The router mounts to an acrylic plastic plate which, in turn, mounts in a cutout in the middle of the holder. Make this cutout with a router and a saber saw.

Clamp three scraps of wood to the worktable stock to form an open-sided square — these scraps will guide the router. The dimensions of this square are determined by the diameter of the router base. You want to rout a groove that forms a square with *outside* dimensions of 8½″ x 8½″. To calculate the *inside* dimensions of the scrap wood square, add the length of a side to the diameter of the router base, and subtract the diameter of the bit. For instance, if you use a ³⁄₄″-diameter bit to cut this groove, and the router base is 7″ across, the inside dimensions of the scrap wood square should be 14³⁄₄″ x 14³⁄₄″ (8½″ plus 7″ minus ³⁄₄″ equals 14³⁄₄″).

Mount a ³⁄₄″-diameter bit in the router and cut the first three sides (right, left, and bottom) of a ³⁄₄″-wide, ³⁄₈″-deep square groove, as shown in the *Holder Layout*. (See Figure 1.) To make the fourth side of the square, remove the three scraps. Re-secure one of them on the holder so that the scrap straddles the grooves you just cut, as shown in Figure 2. Rout the last side (top) of the square.

Mark the bottom of the groove for the cutout, and cut along the line with a saber saw. (See Figure 3.) When you've finished, the cutout should be 7½″ square, and there should be a ½″-wide, ³⁄₈″-deep rabbet all around the perimeter.

Note: It seems logical to make the cutout first, *then* rout the rabbet. But if you follow the procedure given here, the router is easier to control because its entire base is supported when you cut the groove.

1/Because the router plate is placed close to the edge of the holder, you won't be able to cut the square groove in one step. Instead, rout the sides and bottom of the square groove first. Clamp three scraps to the holder to guide the router, and keep the router base pressed against these scraps as you cut. Make several passes, cutting just ¹⁄₁₆″–¹⁄₈″ deeper with each pass.

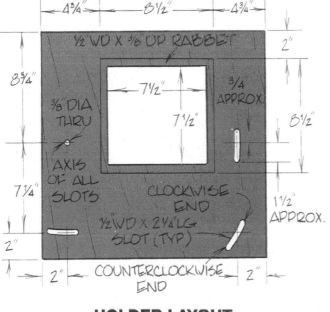

HOLDER LAYOUT

2/Remove the scraps, then re-secure one so it lays across two sides of the square groove, as shown. Rout the top of the groove, using the scrap as a guide.

3/Mark the bottom of the groove where you want to make the cutout. Drill ¹⁄₃″-diameter holes through the waste to start the cuts, then make the cutout with a saber saw.

3 **Drill holes in the holder and mount.**
Place the holder on top of the mount so the sides and bottom edges are flush. Tape the two parts together to keep them from shifting, and mark the positions of the ³/₈″ holes on the mount. Drill all four of these holes through both the mount *and* the holder.

4 **Cut the slots in the holder.** Three of the holes in the holder are enlarged to ½″-wide *curved* slots. The one hole that you don't enlarge serves as the pivot point or axis for routing the three slots.

To rout the slots, you first need to make the *Circle-Routing Jig* shown. Cut the jig from a scrap of ¼″ plywood, drill it, and mount it to the base of the router.

Mount a ³/₈″ straight bit in the router, and place a dowel center in the upper left hole — the axis hole — of the holder. Insert the bit in the lower left-hand hole, rotate the arm of the jig until it's over the dowel center, and press down firmly. The dowel center will leave a mark in the underside of the circle-routing jig. Repeat for the two right-hand holes, then drill ³/₈″-diameter holes through the jig at the marks.

Indicate on the holder where you want to begin and end each slot. The length of each slot is not critical, but it should be about 2¼″. Beginning at the hole, plan to cut ³/₄″ toward the *clockwise* end of each slot, and 1½″ toward the *counterclockwise* end, as shown in the *Holder Layout*.

Replace the ³/₈″ straight bit with a ½″ straight bit. Adjust the depth of cut to about ⅛″. Insert a ³/₈″ carriage bolt through both the hole in the jig arm closest to the router and the axis hole in the holder. Secure it with

4/Rout the curved slots using a circle-routing jig. Use the holes in the jig arm and the upper left-hand hole in the holder as pivot points.

a washer and wing nut. Don't make the nut too tight; you must be able to pivot the arm.

Lift the router and jig up off the holder (the plywood arm will flex slightly), turn the router on, then lower it carefully into the lower left-hand hole in the holder. Swing it clockwise ³/₄″, then counterclockwise 1½″, cutting a curved slot about 2¼″ long. (See Figure 4.) Readjust the depth of cut, and cut the slot about ⅛″ deeper. Repeat until you've cut the slot all the way through the holder. Cut the remaining slots in the same manner.

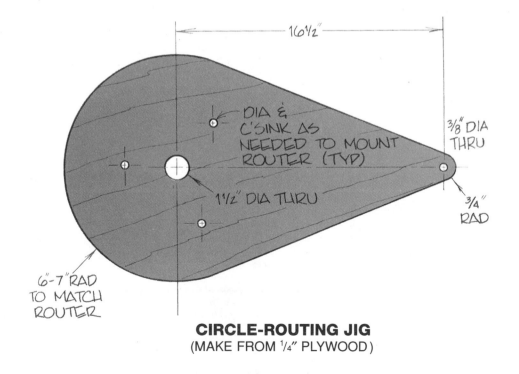

16½″

DIA &
C'SINK AS
NEEDED TO MOUNT
ROUTER (TYP)

³/₈″ DIA
THRU

1½″ DIA THRU

³/₄″
RAD

6″-7″ RAD
TO MATCH
ROUTER

CIRCLE-ROUTING JIG
(MAKE FROM ¼″ PLYWOOD)

5 **Rout the miter gauge groove in the worktable.** Using a router or a dado cutter, rout a groove for a miter gauge in the worktable, as shown in the *Top View* and *Side View*. For most miter gauges, the groove should be 3/4″ wide and 3/8″ deep. However, this measurement may vary depending on the make of the gauge, so check your miter gauge and rout a groove to fit.

6 **Assemble the mortising jig.** Assemble the worktable, mount, base, front, and braces with glue and #8 flathead wood screws. Countersink the heads of the screws slightly below the surface of the wood. As you put the parts together, constantly check that they are square to each other. Sand the joints clean and flush.

7 **Attach cleats to the holder.** To adequately support the router, the rabbet around the perimeter of the cutout must be reinforced. To do this, glue the cleats to the back surface of the holder, as shown in the *Back View*.

8 **Apply a finish to the mortising table.** Apply a finish to all the wooden surfaces of the mortising table. Use a penetrating finish, such as Danish oil or tung oil. Avoid finishes that build up on the surface, such as varnish or polyurethane. Apply several coats of wax to the worktable and the holder — this will help boards glide across them as you use the mortising jig.

9 **Mount the router to the holder.** Using a saber saw, cut a sheet of 3/8″-thick acrylic plastic to fit the cutout in the holder. This will serve as a mounting plate for the router. Drill a 1 1/2″-diameter hole through the center of this plate, as shown in the *Back View*.

Remove the base from the router. Place the acrylic plate on the workbench and center the router on top of it. Mark the position of the base mounting holes on the plate. Remove the router, then drill mounting holes in the plate. Countersink these holes on the front (working) surface. Also drill and countersink 1/8″-diameter pilot holes at the corners of the plate to mount it to the holder.

Mount the acrylic plate to the holder with flathead wood screws. The front surface of the plate must be precisely flush with that of the holder, and the screws should be slightly below the surface. Using the same machine screws that hold the base to the router, attach the router to the back side of the acrylic plate. Once again, the heads of these bolts should be slightly below the surface of the plastic.

10 **Mount the holder on the worktable assembly.** Insert carriage bolts through all four holes in the mounts. Place the holder over these bolts, put flat washers and wing nuts on the bolts, then hand-tighten the wing nuts.

To use the router mortising jig, clamp the base to your workbench so the mount hangs over the edge of the work surface. Mount a bit in the router and adjust the depth of cut as you would normally. To adjust the height of the bit above the worktable, loosen the wing nuts, pivot the holder clockwise or counterclockwise, then tighten the nuts.

Tips for Using the Router Mortising Jig

When using the router mortising jig, be careful not to let your hands stray too close to the bit – keep them at least 2″ away at all times. To provide a visual reminder, paint a red "danger zone" on the worktable, 4″ wide and 4″ deep, centered under the bit.

Here are some additional tips for using the jig safely:

When making plunge cuts or routing deep grooves, dadoes, and similar joints, use spiral router bits. These clear the chips from the cut faster than ordinary straight bits, and keep the bit from heating up. They're available through most mail-order woodworking suppliers.

When routing mortises and other blind joints, you must know where to begin and end the cuts. Stick a piece of masking tape to the mounting plate just above the bit. Then use a square to mark the diameter of the bit on the tape. Start a cut or stop it when these diameter marks line up with the layout marks on the workpiece.

To make a plunge cut, simply drill a hole by moving the wood into the bit. If accuracy is important, clamp a straightedge to the worktable to guide the wood.

Except when making plunge cuts, always feed the work into the bit so the rotation helps hold it down on the table. Since most routers rotate counterclockwise (as you face the mounting plate), feed the work from right to left. You may want to paint an arrow on the worktable for a visual reminder.

Perfectly Flat Materials

Worktables, jigs, and fixtures often must be built of an especially flat, even material that does not expand, shrink, or warp over time. For example, if the worktable of a router cabinet is not perfectly flat, or if it changes shape after you build it, then you will have great difficulty turning out accurate work. Solid wood, even kiln-dried hardwoods, won't do because all solid wood changes shape over time. There are, however, several special materials that are perfectly flat and retain that flatness — and you can cut them with woodworking tools.

MDF Board — "MDF" stands for Medium Density Fiberboard. It's available on special order through most lumberyards and building supply centers. When you work with it, you'll find its name is something of a misnomer. The fiber is extremely dense and fine — so fine that cutting and routing leave a perfectly smooth edge, unlike ordinary fiberboard. Of all the flat materials, this is probably the flattest and the most stable — it will not expand, contract, or warp. The trade-off is that it's not especially strong or durable. It will flex slightly and the surface is easily scratched or gouged. (MDF is *not* tempered, like some fiberboards.) It should be braced or backed up with more durable materials.

Sink Cutouts — When cabinetmakers cut holes in countertops for sinks, they often recycle the cutouts at building supply centers, which in turn sell them for as little as $1 apiece. These large pieces (about 20″ x 30″) of laminate-covered particleboard make excellent worktables because they are very stable and remain relatively flat. The laminate is extremely hard and resists scratches and gouges. It's also very smooth and produces little friction when you feed a board across it. However, these cutouts will bend and break easily, particularly if you cut them into long, narrow strips. Brace them with stronger materials. They're also very hard on cutting tools. Feed them slowly into blades, knives, and bits. When routing, take very shallow bites with each pass.

Note: If you need a worktable larger than 20″ x 30″, you can buy an entire countertop — but you won't get it for $1.

Baltic Birch Plywood — This plywood is imported from Scandinavia and the Soviet Union. It's not available through every lumberyard, even on special order. You may have to call around to find the regional distributor nearest you, or purchase it through a mail-order woodworking supply company. Because of the way in which this plywood is made, it's much flatter and more stable than ordinary cabinet-grade plywood. It's also very strong, and is difficult to break. Finally, it comes in many different thicknesses, from ⅛″ to 1⅛″. Its only drawbacks are that it does bend — particularly the thinner stock — and the surface is soft.

Laminated Maple — Several wood-product companies make laminated maple countertops. As with Baltic birch, you may have to call around to find a regional distributor. Be prepared for sticker shock — a 60″-long countertop sells for well over $100, retail. These countertops are usually 1⅛″ or 1¼″ thick, and are composed of narrow strips of hard maple glued together to make a single board 24″–25″ wide. They're planed and sanded flat, then sealed so they stay that way. They're extremely strong and durable, but not as stable as the other materials on this list. To keep them from changing shape, seal them as soon as possible after you cut or shape them.

If you need a flat, stable material *to make a worktable or a jig, here are four choices: (1) laminated hard maple, (2) MDF board, (3) Baltic birch plywood, and (4) a sink cutout of laminate-covered particleboard.*

Double-Support Sawhorses

Few woodworking aids are handier than a pair of sawhorses. They will support almost anything for almost any operation. You can lay a board across them while crosscutting, use them when applying a finish to projects, and even employ them as legs for a tabletop should you need some extra work space. But for all of the service they give, conventional sawhorses don't provide as much support as they might. A few inches out from the rail, the boards begin to bend and flex.

The sawhorses shown provide much more support than the ordinary variety. Instead of one rail, they each have two, spaced a short distance apart. This provides a "sawing well" when you cut a board — the double rails support *both* sides of the cut. There is less binding, splintering, and chipping. Consequently, the work seems easier and you get better cuts.

In addition, the sawhorses can be linked with two cross rails, providing support *between* the horses. The rails and the cross rails are joined with lap joints, and both parts are notched so that you can place the horses close together or far apart, depending on what you have to support and how much support you need. ●

Materials List

FINISHED DIMENSIONS

PARTS

A. Legs (8) $1\frac{1}{2}$" x $3\frac{1}{2}$" x $24\frac{13}{16}$"
B. Rails (4) $1\frac{1}{2}$" x $5\frac{1}{2}$" x 48"
C. Gussets (8) $\frac{3}{4}$" x 8" x $10\frac{1}{2}$"
D. End spacers (4) $1\frac{1}{2}$" x 3" x $10\frac{3}{4}$"
E. End braces (4) $1\frac{1}{2}$" x $3\frac{1}{2}$" x $10\frac{3}{4}$"
F. Cross rails (2) $1\frac{1}{2}$" x $3\frac{1}{2}$" x 96"

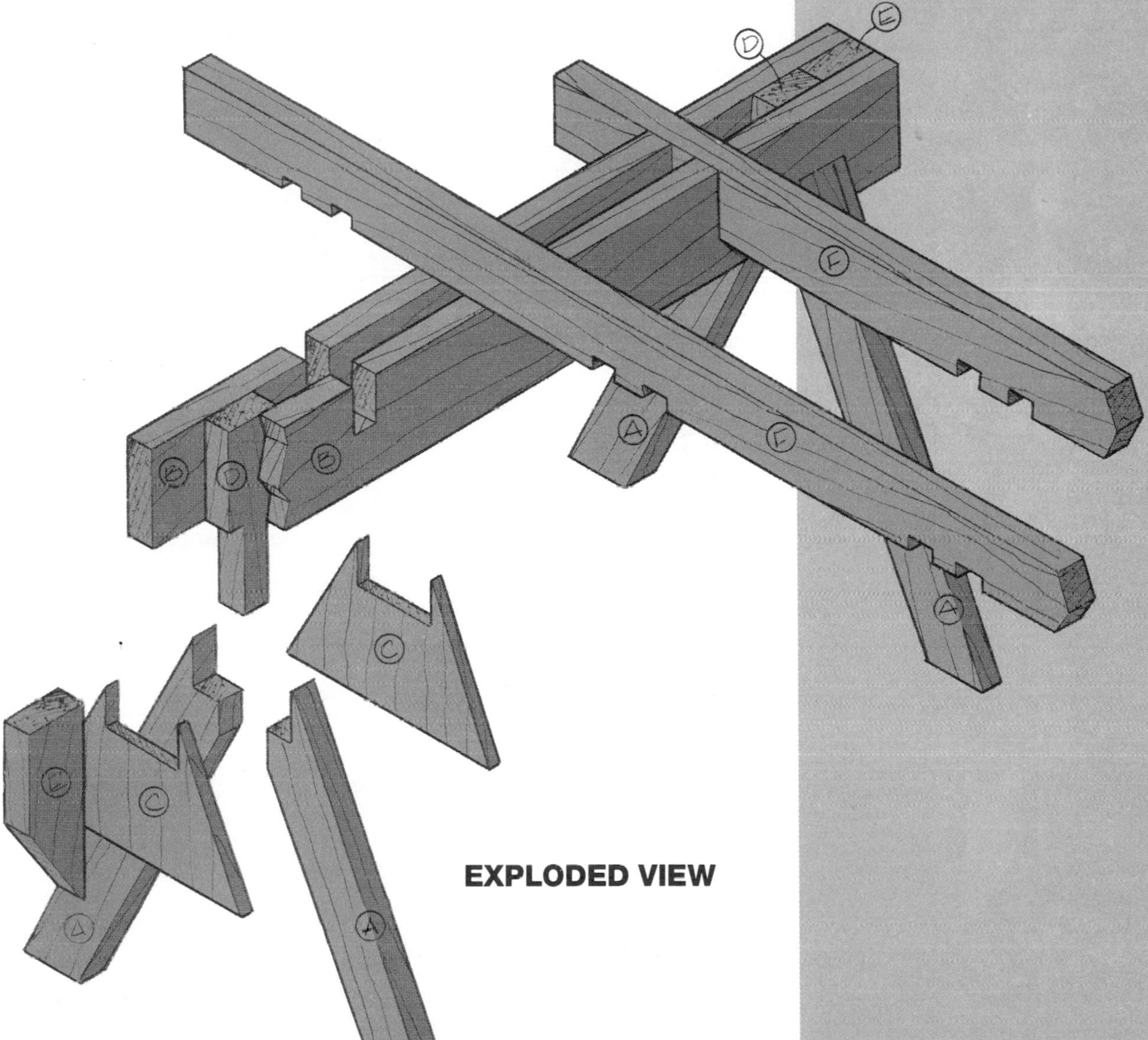

EXPLODED VIEW

HARDWARE

16d Galvanized nails ($\frac{1}{4}$ lb.)
8d Galvanized nails ($\frac{1}{4}$ lb.)

1 **Cut the parts to size.** To make this project, you need two 2 x 6s, each 8′ long, five 2 x 4s, each 10′ long, and some scraps of ¾″ plywood. Choose clear stock; knots will weaken the sawhorse, especially if they happen to fall in the vicinity of the notches. Cut all the parts to the sizes specified in the Materials List. As you cut, miter the bottom ends of the legs and braces, as shown in the *Leg Layout* and *End Brace Layout*.

2 **Cut the shapes of the legs, end spacers, and gussets.** Lay out the shapes of the legs, end spacers, and gussets on the stock, as shown in the *Leg Layout, End Spacer Layout,* and *Gusset Layout*. Cut the shapes with a band saw or saber saw.

3 **Cut the lap joints in the rails and cross rails.** The cross rails rest in 1½″-wide, 2¾″-deep notches in the rails. To make these notches, line up all the rails, face to face and top edge up, on your workbench. Make sure the ends are all flush. Clamp the rails together with bar clamps to keep them from shifting.

Measure and mark the locations of the notches on one rail, then transfer these marks across the other parts with a carpenter's square.

Using a hand saw, cut the faces of the notches, sawing across all the rails. (See Figure 1.) Knock the waste out of the notches with a wide chisel. (See Figure 2.) The notches in all the rails will be cut to exactly the same depth and width, and will be spaced precisely the same as well. Repeat this procedure for the cross rails, making 1½″-wide, ¾″ deep notches as shown in the *Cross Rail Layout*.

1/Clamp the rails together in order to saw the notches in all of them at the same time.

2/With the rails still clamped together, remove the waste from the notches with a chisel.

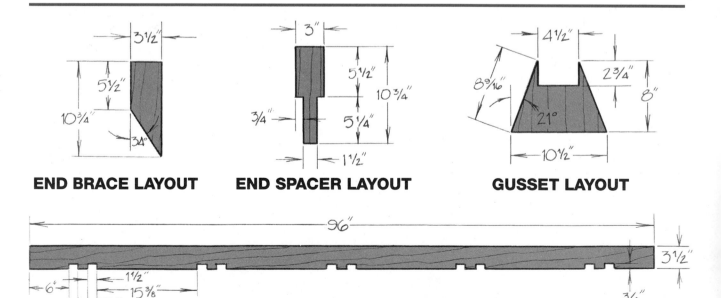

END BRACE LAYOUT

END SPACER LAYOUT

GUSSET LAYOUT

CROSS RAIL LAYOUT

4

Assemble the sawhorses. Lay a gusset on a flat surface, then arrange two legs and an end spacer on it. Prop up the bottom ends of the legs with ³⁄₄"-thick scraps. Place another gusset over the parts and attach it to the legs and spacer with 8d nails. Turn the assembly over and attach the other gusset. Repeat for the other three pairs of legs.

Assemble the rails and braces with 16d nails — be careful that the notches are lined up properly. Slide the leg assemblies in place and attach them to the rail assemblies with 16d nails.

To use the sawhorses, stand them up and position them so they're parallel. Line up the notches on the cross rails with the notches on one set of sawhorse rails and put them together. Align the second sawhorse so that the cross rail drops into place.

Warning: Do *not* stand on these sawhorses or use them to support scaffolding.

TRY THIS! If you don't want to line up the rail and cross rail notches every time you use these sawhorses, you can substitute 1½" x 2¾" x 96" boards with *no* notches for the cross rails. Simply drop these into the rail notches anywhere you want to. This is much quicker. However, you give up a lot of rigidity — and a little support.

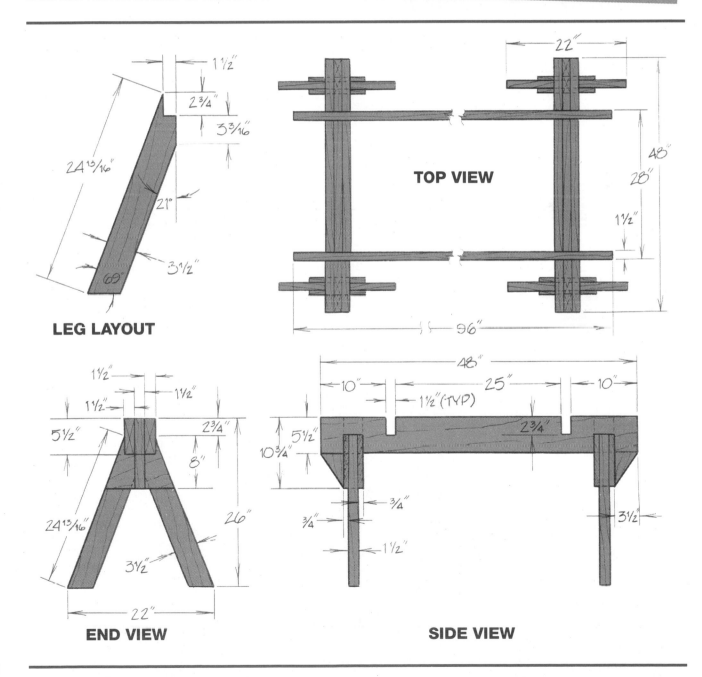

LEG LAYOUT

TOP VIEW

END VIEW

SIDE VIEW

Clamping Aids

To accomplish a particular clamping operation, you sometimes need more than just clamps. Here are three quick-and-easy *clamping aids* to help get your projects together properly before the glue begins to set.

This *pipe clamp holder* keeps the pipes from rolling while you glue stock edge to edge. It also keeps glue from squeezing out of the joints and dripping on your workbench. This helps save clean-up time.

The *corner squares* hold two pieces of wood at right angles to each other while you clamp them together. They are particularly useful for gluing up table aprons, drawers, and frames of all sorts.

The *bench jack* is a simple jig with dozens of different uses. Its original purpose was to hold a board on edge for planing, but it can also be used to hold small parts vertical while you mark, saw, drill, or sand them. ✹

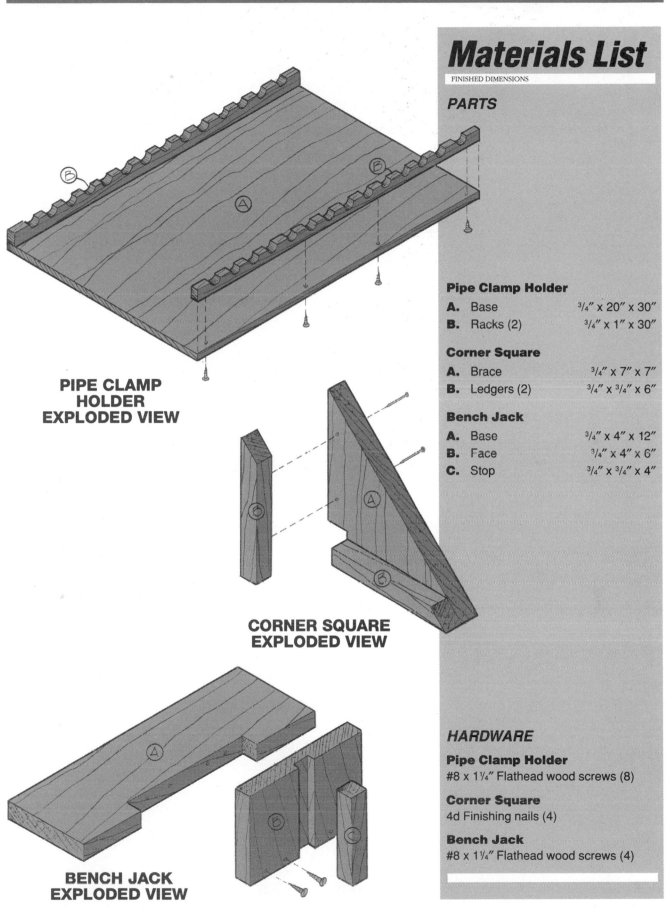

Materials List

FINISHED DIMENSIONS

PARTS

Pipe Clamp Holder
A. Base   3/4" x 20" x 30"
B. Racks (2)   3/4" x 1" x 30"

Corner Square
A. Brace   3/4" x 7" x 7"
B. Ledgers (2) 3/4" x 3/4" x 6"

Bench Jack
A. Base   3/4" x 4" x 12"
B. Face   3/4" x 4" x 6"
C. Stop   3/4" x 3/4" x 4"

HARDWARE

Pipe Clamp Holder
#8 x 1¼" Flathead wood screws (8)

Corner Square
4d Finishing nails (4)

Bench Jack
#8 x 1¼" Flathead wood screws (4)

**PIPE CLAMP
HOLDER
EXPLODED VIEW**

**CORNER SQUARE
EXPLODED VIEW**

**BENCH JACK
EXPLODED VIEW**

Making the Pipe Clamp Holder

1 ***Select the stock and cut the parts to size.*** To make this project, you need a scrap of hardwood such as birch, maple, or oak, and a laminate-covered sink cutout. These cutouts are available at most building supply centers, although these stores won't always have them in stock. If you can't find a cutout,

contact a cabinetmaker and ask him to save you one the next time he installs a kitchen cabinet with a double sink.

Cut the base to the sizes shown in the Materials List, and cut one piece of stock 2⅛" wide and 30" long to make the racks.

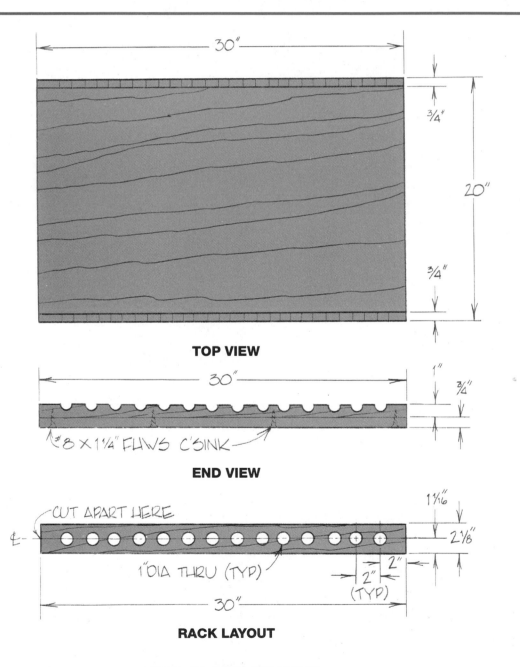

TOP VIEW

END VIEW

RACK LAYOUT

PIPE CLAMP HOLDER

2

Make the racks. Mark the center of the rack stock, then drill 1″-diameter holes through it every 2″, as shown in the *Rack Layout*. Rip the rack stock in half to make two pieces, each 1″ wide. (See Figure 1.)

1/After drilling a line of evenly spaced 1″-diameter holes through the rack stock, rip it in half. Both pieces will have half-round scallops in one edge.

3

Assemble and finish the holder. Sand the racks and apply a finish. Attach the racks to the laminated side of the base with screws. (Don't bother to glue the racks in place — wood glue won't stick to the laminate.) Countersink the screws so the heads are flush with the bottom surface of the base. Apply several coats of wax to the completed project to prevent glue from adhering to it.

Making the Corner Square

1

Select the stock and cut the parts to size. To make this project, you need a few scraps of hardwood and ¾″ cabinet-grade plywood. When you have gathered the stock, cut the ledgers to size and miter the ends at 45°. Cut the plywood into 7″ x 7″ squares.

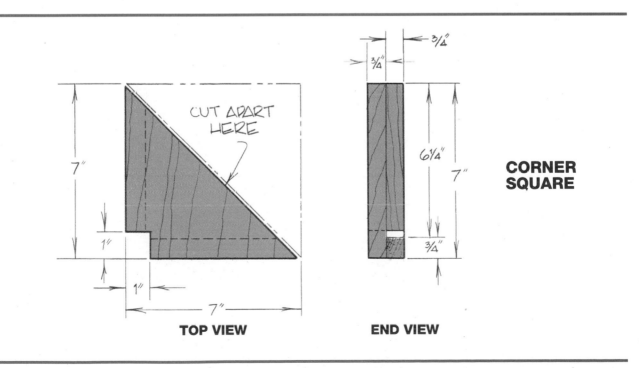

CUT APART HERE

7″

1″

1″

7″

TOP VIEW

¾″

¾″

6¼″

7″

¾″

END VIEW

CORNER SQUARE

2

Cut the braces. Using a band saw or table saw, cut the plywood squares in half diagonally to make right triangles. To do this safely and accurately on the table saw, make a simple jig that will hold the squares while you cut them. (See Figure 2.)

Using a band saw, cut 1″-wide, 1″-deep notches in the 90° corner of each brace.

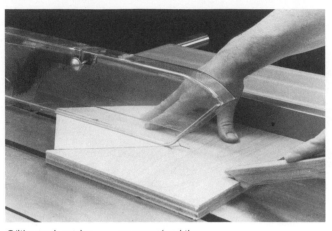

2/It's much easier (and safer) to cut each plywood square with the aid of a jig. Nail two strips to a scrap of plywood to hold the squares at the proper angle to the blade. Feed the *squares (and the jig) into the blade, using the fence to guide the jig. Be careful not to cut all the way through the jig — and don't hit a nail.* **Sawguard removed for clarity.**

3

Assemble and finish the corner squares. Finish sand the ledgers. Glue the ledgers to the triangles, and reinforce them with finishing nails. Set the heads of the nails. When the glue dries, sand the joints clean and flush. (See Figure 3.) Apply a finish and several coats of wax to prevent glue from sticking to the completed corner squares.

3/When you sand the joints of the corner squares, remember that the ledgers must be precisely 90° from *each other. If you have a disk sander or a belt sander, use a miter gauge to maintain this angle.*

Making the Bench Jack

1

Select the stock and cut the parts to size. To make this project, you need several hardwood scraps — the harder the better. The jack shown is made from birch, but you can also use hard maple or oak. When you have selected the stock, cut the parts to the sizes shown in the Materials List.

2

Cut the joinery. To hold the face in the base, cut a 6″-long, 3/4″-deep notch in one edge of the base. This notch must be centered in the base, 3″ from either end. Using a router or a dado cutter, cut a 3/4″-wide, 3/8″-deep dado in the face. This joint, too, should be centered, 2⅝″ from either end.

3

Assemble and finish the bench jack. Finish sand the parts. Glue the stop in the face dado, then glue the face to the base. Make sure the face is precisely 90° from the base. Reinforce the face-to-base glue joint with flathead wood screws. Countersink the screws so their heads are flush with the surface of the face. Sand the joints clean and flush, then apply a finish and several coats of wax to the completed bench jack.

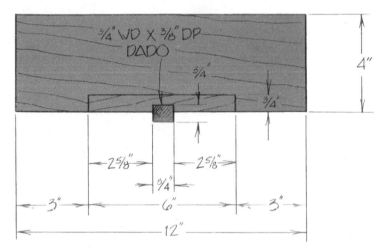

TOP VIEW

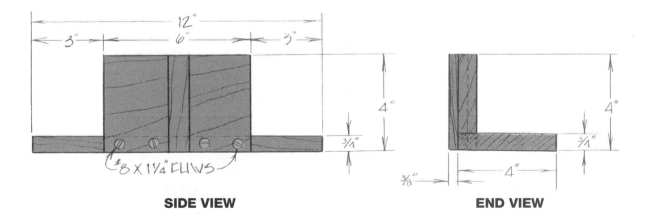

SIDE VIEW   **END VIEW**

BENCH JACK

Table Saw Cutoff Box

While a table saw is a precise cutting tool, the miter gauge doesn't offer enough support to hold a long board securely. Consequently, the piece may move or twist as you cut it, and the cutoff edge or end won't be square.

A cutoff box solves this problem. It holds long, wide workpieces precisely 90° to the saw blade while you cut them. Use it in the same manner as a miter gauge — mount the box in the miter gauge slots, place a board against the face, then slide the box forward into the blade. The large sliding table and long face provide much more support than you can get from a miter gauge — even a miter gauge with an extension fence.

This particular cutoff box offers several extra features. The face is adjustable, letting you align it precisely with the saw blade. Several push-action clamps hold the workpiece while you cut it. If you don't need the clamps, or if the clamp bar is in the way of your work, you can easily remove it from the box. ✸

Materials List

FINISHED DIMENSIONS

PARTS

A.	Sliding table*	$^3/_4$" x 21$^1/_2$" x 30"
B.	Guide bars (2)	$^3/_8$" x $^3/_4$" x 21$^1/_2$"
C.	Faces (2)	$^3/_4$" x 5" x 30"
D.	Bases (2)	$^3/_4$" x 2" x 30"
E.	Braces (14)	$^3/_4$" x 2" x 4$^1/_4$"
F.	Clamp bar	1$^1/_2$" x 3" x 28"

*Make this from plywood or MDF board.

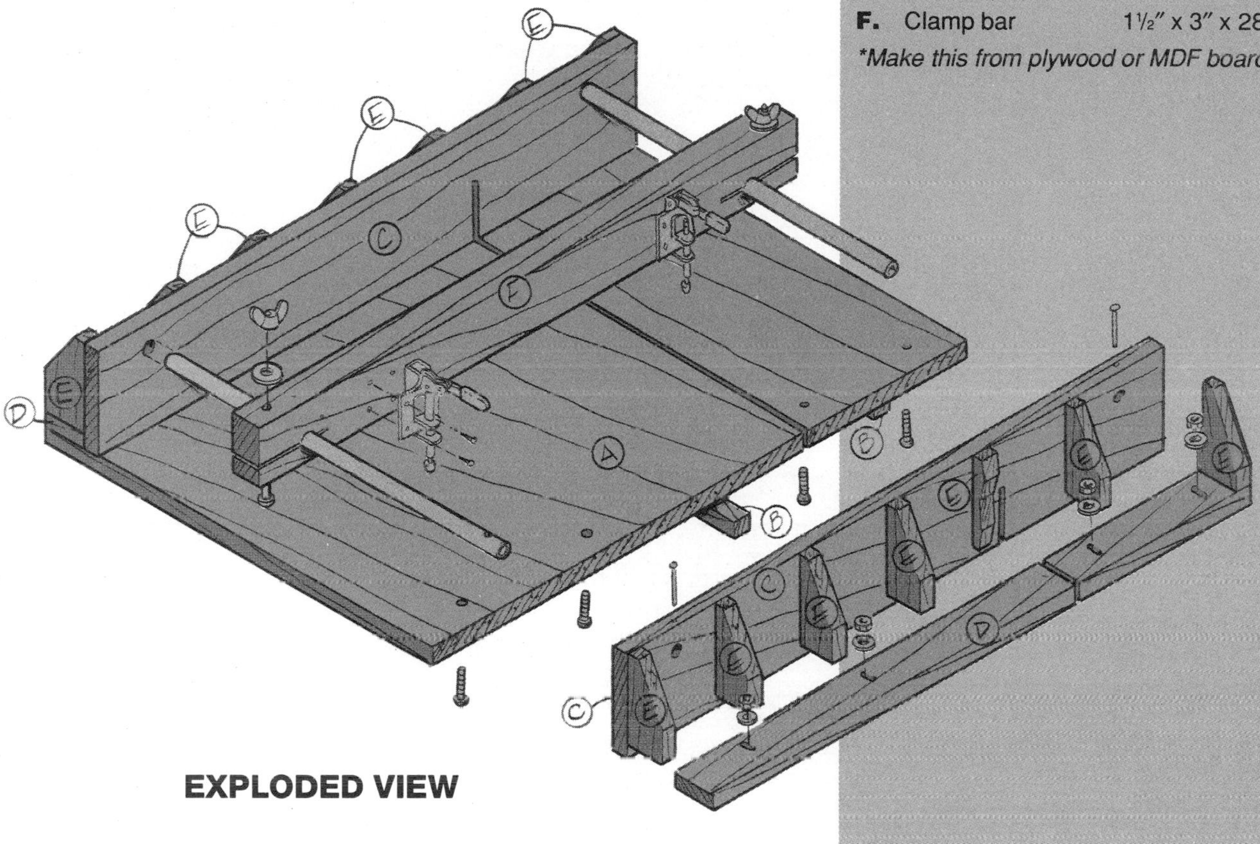

EXPLODED VIEW

HARDWARE

#8 x 1$^1/_4$" Flathead wood screws (48–60)
1" Wire brads (16–24)
$^3/_8$" x 3$^1/_2$" Carriage bolts (2)
$^1/_4$" x 2" Carriage bolts (10)
$^3/_8$" Flat washers (2)
$^1/_4$" Flat washers (8)
$^3/_8$" Wing nuts (2)
$^1/_4$" Hex nuts (8)
$^3/_4$"-dia. x 18$^1/_2$" Steel rods or pipes (2)
Push-action clamps and mounting screws (2)

1 Inspect and measure your table saw.

As designed, this cutoff box will fit most 10″ table saws with table extensions. Carefully measure your saw to see if the box will work for you as is. If not, adjust the measurements so it will.

Also give some thought to the positions of the guide bars, carriage bolts, and braces. When you mount the finished cutoff box on your saw and push it forward into the blade, cutting the ⅛″-wide kerf shown in the *Top View,* the blade must *not* slice through a brace or a carriage bolt. If the braces or bolts shown in the drawings are positioned incorrectly for your saw, move them.

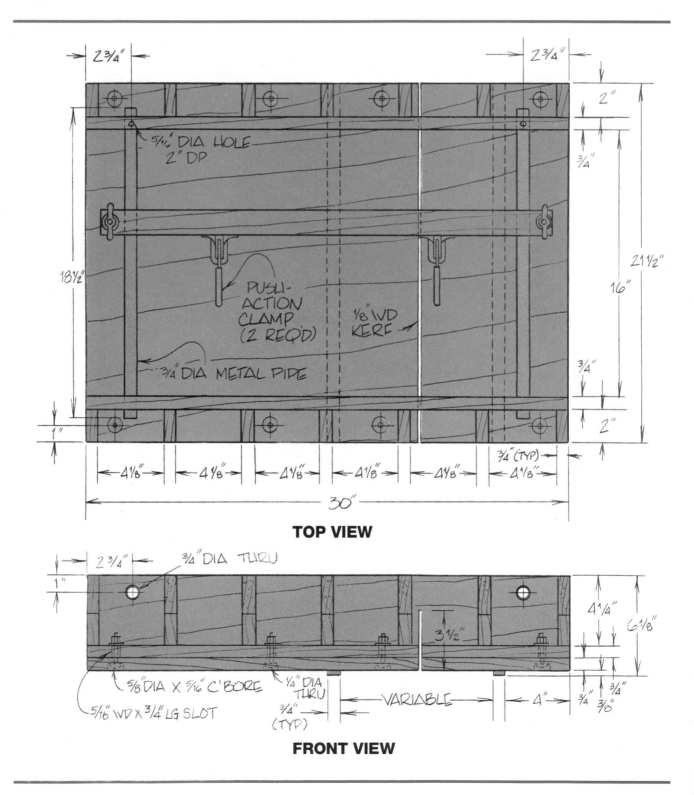

TOP VIEW

FRONT VIEW

2

Select the stock and cut the parts to size. To build this project, you need approximately 4 board feet of 4/4 (four-quarters) stock, a scrap of 8/4 (eight-quarters) stock, and a 4' x 4' sheet of ¾" plywood or particleboard. This sheet must be very flat, such as Baltic birch plywood, MDF board, or laminate-covered particleboard. The wood should be very hard, such as maple, birch, or oak. The cutoff box shown is made from MDF board, Baltic birch plywood, and birch. When you have gathered the materials, cut them to the sizes needed.

3

Drill the holes needed. Lay out the locations of the holes on the various parts. Most of these holes must be placed accurately, so measure carefully. The positions of the counterbores and bolt holes in the sliding table are not critical, but they should be spaced evenly. They must also not interfere with the braces or saw kerf. After measuring, drill the following holes in the components:

- ¾"-diameter holes through the faces of the clamp bar, as shown in the *Clamp Bar/Front View,* to mount it on the steel pipes
- ¾"-diameter holes through the faces, as shown in the *Front View,* to hold the steel pipes
- ⅝"-diameter, ⁵⁄₁₆"-deep counterbores in the underside of the sliding table, for carriage bolts
- ¼"-diameter holes through the counterbores
- ⅜"-diameter holes through the edges of the clamp bar, as shown in the *Clamp Bar/Top View,* for carriage bolts
- ⁵⁄₁₆"-diameter, 2"-deep holes in the edges of *one* face, to pin the steel pipes in place, as shown in the *Top View*
- ⁵⁄₁₆"-diameter holes through the steel rods or pipes, as shown in the *Pipe Hole Detail,* for the pins

4

Cut the slots in the bases. The bases are slotted, allowing you to move them slightly and square them to the blade. Space these ⁵⁄₁₆" wide, ¾" long slots so they line up with the bolt holes in the sliding table. Make each slot by drilling a line of ⁵⁄₁₆"-diameter holes, then cleaning up the edges with a chisel.

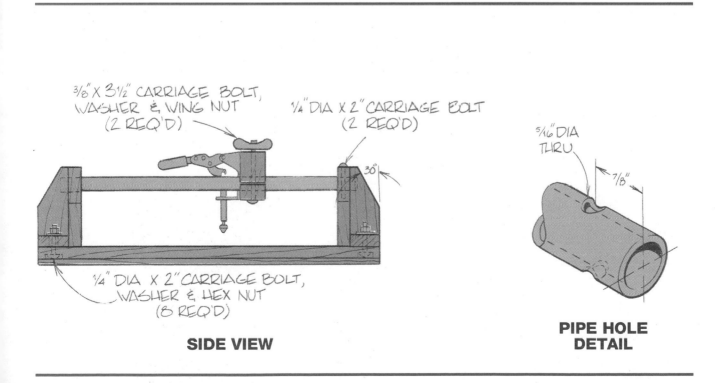

³⁄₈" X 3½" CARRIAGE BOLT, WASHER & WING NUT (2 REQ'D)

¼" DIA X 2" CARRIAGE BOLT (2 REQ'D)

5/16" DIA THRU

7/8"

30°

¼" DIA X 2" CARRIAGE BOLT, WASHER & HEX NUT (8 REQ'D)

SIDE VIEW

PIPE HOLE DETAIL

5

Cut slots in the clamp bar. Using a table saw or a band saw, cut a ⅛″-wide, 3″-long kerf through each ¾″-diameter hole in the clamp bar, as shown in the *Clamp Bar/Front View*. These slots allow you to secure the clamp bar to the steel pipes.

6

Attach the guide bars to the sliding table. Place the guide bars in the miter gauge slots. They should be flush with the table surface and slide easily. If they bind, remove a little stock with a scraper or sander. If they're too loose, remake them.

Lower the blade completely. Put the sliding table on the table saw worktable and position it over the guide bars as shown in the *Front View*. Mark the position of each guide bar on the front and back edge of the sliding table. Remove the table and put a line of glue on each guide. Replace the table, lining up the marks with the guides, front and back.

Drive four brads through the sliding table and into the guide bars to hold them in place. (Don't seat the brads; you'll remove them later.) Remove the sliding table from the table saw and wipe any glue off the tool.

Turn the sliding table upside down. Tack the guides to the table with brads, and set the heads. Remove the brads from the top side of the table. Let the glue dry, then lightly sand the guides clean.

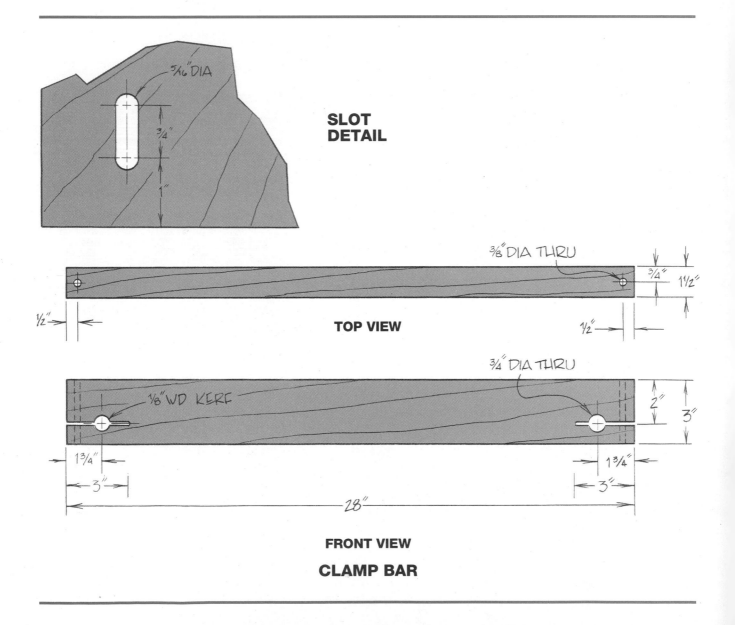

SLOT DETAIL

⁵⁄₁₆″ DIA

¾″

1″

⅜″ DIA THRU

¾″

1½″

TOP VIEW

½″

½″

¾″ DIA THRU

⅛″ WD KERF

2″

3″

1¾″

3″

28″

1¾″

3″

FRONT VIEW

CLAMP BAR

7

Assemble the cutoff box. Miter one corner of each brace at 30°, as shown in the *Side View*. Sand the sawed edges, then finish sand all the parts of the cutoff box. Assemble the faces, bases, and braces with glue and screws. Countersink the screws so the heads are slightly below the surface. Let the glue dry, then sand all joints clean and flush.

Insert ¼" x 2" carriage bolts up through the holes in the sliding table. Place the face/base assemblies over the bolts and secure them with flat washers and hex nuts. Do *not* tighten the nuts.

Drill several sets of pilot holes for the push-action clamps along the length of the bar — one set every 2" — so you can move the clamps around as needed. Attach the clamps to the clamp bar with screws.

Insert ⅜" x 3½" carriage bolts up through the holes in the clamp bar. Put flat washers and wing nuts on the ends of each bolt, but do *not* tighten the nuts. Insert the pipes through the ¾"-diameter holes in one face, through the holes in the clamp bar, and through the holes in the second face. Line up the 5/16"-diameter holes in the pipe with those in the edge of the face, and drop ¼" x 2" carriage bolts into these holes. These bolts will pin the pipes in the box. When you need to remove the clamp bar and pipes, simply lift the pins out of the holes.

When you use the clamps, slide the clamp bar back and forth over the work to position the clamps wherever you need them. (You can make more clamp bars if this one isn't enough.) To secure the clamps, tighten the wing nuts at either end of the clamp bar.

Place the cutoff box on your table saw, fitting the guide bars into the miter gauge slots. Pull the box back toward you, exposing the blade. Raise the blade as far as it will go, turn the saw on, then slowly push the box through the blade. Cut a ⅛"-wide kerf through the sliding table and partway through the face/base assemblies. Make sure the blade doesn't hit a screw or carriage bolt!

8

Finish the cutoff box. Remove the pipes and clamp bar from the faces. Detach the faces from the sliding table and remove all the hardware. Do any necessary touch-up sanding, and apply a finish to the wooden parts. Wax the guide bars and *bottom* surface of the table so it will slide smoothly across the table saw. Then reassemble the components of the cutoff box.

9

Align the cutoff box. Place the box on the saw, with the blade raised to its full height. Unplug the saw so you don't turn it on accidentally. Using a square, align each face 90° from the saw blade. (See Figure 1.) Tighten the hex nuts that hold the bases to the table, securing the alignment. When you place a board in the cutoff box and clamp it against a face, it should be perfectly square to the blade.

Warning: To use this cutoff box, you must remove the saw guard from the table. When you do this, be extremely careful. Adjust the saw blade height as low as possible for each cut. While you're cutting, do *not* put your hand inside the box.

1/To align the faces with the saw blade, first make sure all the hex nuts are loose. Place one arm of a square on a face, and the other on the side of the blade. **Make sure the square doesn't touch the blade teeth.** Position the face so it's square to the blade and tighten the hex nuts. Repeat for the other face.

Hanging Cabinets

If you store many small tools and materials in your workshop, these hanging cabinets offer some distinct advantages.

They will hold the items at eye level, where you can see and reach them easily. You can hang items at the back of each cabinet or on each door. You can also set them on shelves. By drilling holes or cutting notches in the fronts of the shelves, you can create racks for screwdrivers, chisels, router bits, and similar tools. The heights of the shelves are easily adjustable, to accommodate the items you want to store.

The cabinets are easy to build — they're just large, plywood boxes with doors. And they're designed to be easily mass-produced. You can make three or four of them almost as easily as you can make one, and line them up side by side on your workshop wall.

Finally, they're easy to install. Simply drive screws through the mounting rail at the back of each cabinet and into the frame studs in your shop wall.

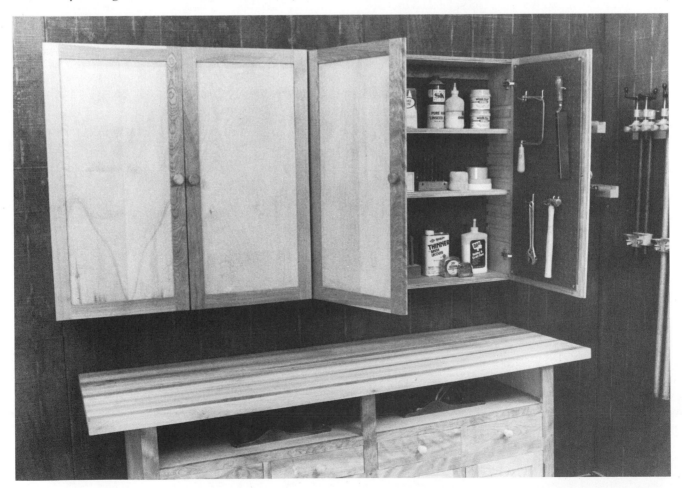

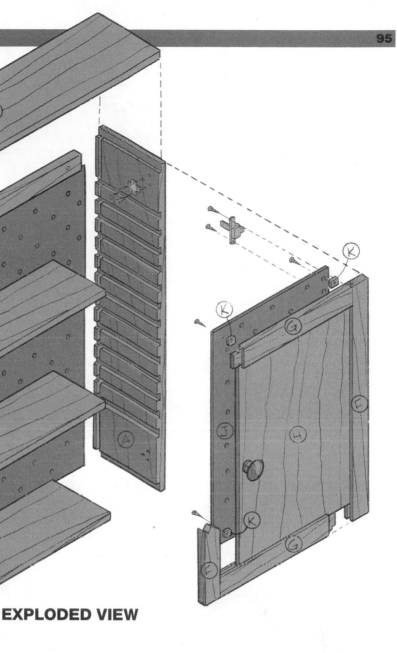

EXPLODED VIEW

Materials List

FINISHED DIMENSIONS

PARTS

A. Sides* (2)   ³/₄″ x 8″ x 36

B. Top/bottom* (2)   ³/₄″ x 8″ x 35¹/₄″

C. Mounting rail**   ³/₄″ x 2″ x 34¹/₂″

D. Back*** ¹/₄″ x 33¹/₄″ x 35¹/₄″

E. Shelves**
(2–4)   ³/₄″ x (variable) x 35¹/₈″

F. Door stiles** (4)   ³/₄″ x 2″ x 36″

G. Door rails** (4) ³/₄″ x 2″ x 15¹⁵/₁₆″

H. Door
panels* (2)   ¹/₄″ x 14⁵/₈″ x 32⁵/₈″

J. Door
backs*** (2)   ¹/₄″ x 15¹⁵/₁₆″ x 34″

K. Spacers** (8)   ¹/₄″ x ³/₄″ x ³/₄″

*Make from cabinet-grade plywood.
**Make from solid wood.
***Make from pegboard.

HARDWARE

95° Full overlay European-style
   cabinet hinges (4)

Door pulls (2)

#8 x 1¹/₄″ Flathead wood screws (16)

#10 x 1″ Roundhead wood screws (8)

#10 Flat washers (8)

¹/₄″ x 3″ Lag screws (2)

¹/₄″ Flat washers (2)

1

Select the stock and cut the parts to size. To make each cabinet, you need about 6–10 board feet of solid wood, a 4' x 4' sheet of ¾" cabinet-grade plywood, a 4' x 4' sheet of ¼" cabinet-grade plywood, and a 4' x 6' sheet of ¼" pegboard. The exact amount of solid wood will depend on how many shelves you make for the cabinet. Select a very hard

wood, such as birch, maple, or oak, and plywood with a matching veneer. The cabinet shown was made from birch and birch-veneer plywood.

After you've selected the materials, cut the parts to the sizes shown in the Materials List, except the shelves. Wait until after you've built and hung the cabinet before you make the shelves.

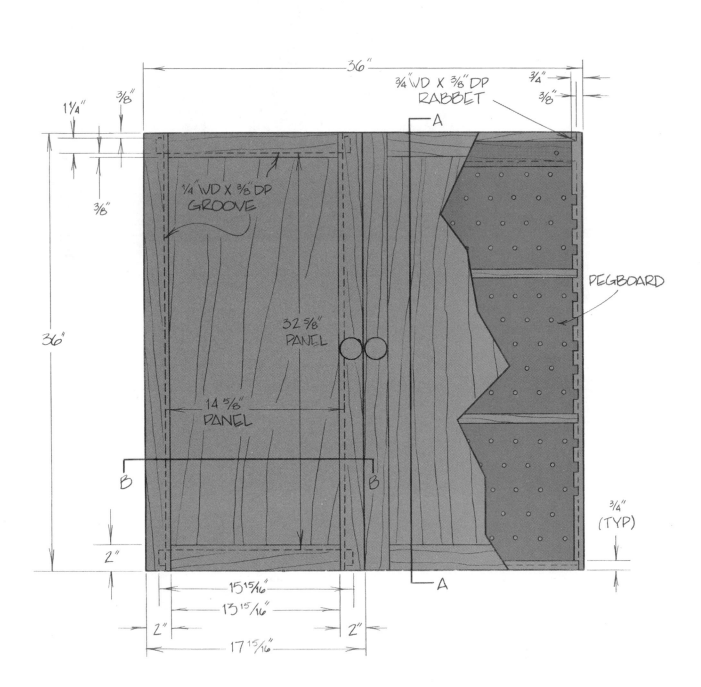

FRONT VIEW

2

Cut the joinery needed to assemble the cabinet case and doors. The cabinet is assembled with simple dadoes, rabbets, and grooves, and the doors with haunched mortises and tenons. The tool setups required to make these joints are similar, so it's easiest to cut all the joinery at the same time. Use a router or a dado cutter to cut the following joints:

- ³⁄₄″-wide, ³⁄₈″-deep rabbets in the sides, as shown in the *Side Layout,* to hold the top and bottom
- ³⁄₄″-wide, ³⁄₈″-deep dadoes in the sides to hold the adjustable shelves
- ¹⁄₄″-wide, ³⁄₈″-deep grooves in the sides and bottom to hold the back

- ¹⁄₄″-wide, ³⁄₈″-deep groove in the bottom edge of the mounting rail to hold the back
- ¹⁄₄″-wide, ³⁄₈″-deep grooves in the inside edges of the door stiles and rails
- ¹⁄₄″-wide, 1″-deep (as measured from the inside edge), 1¹⁄₄″-long mortises in the stiles, ³⁄₈″ from either end, as shown in the *Door Joinery Detail*
- ¹⁄₄″-thick, 1″-long tenons on the ends of the rails

Using a band saw or a dovetail saw, cut a ⁵⁄₈″-wide, ³⁄₈″-deep notch in the tenons to create a "haunch." This will fit them to their mortises.

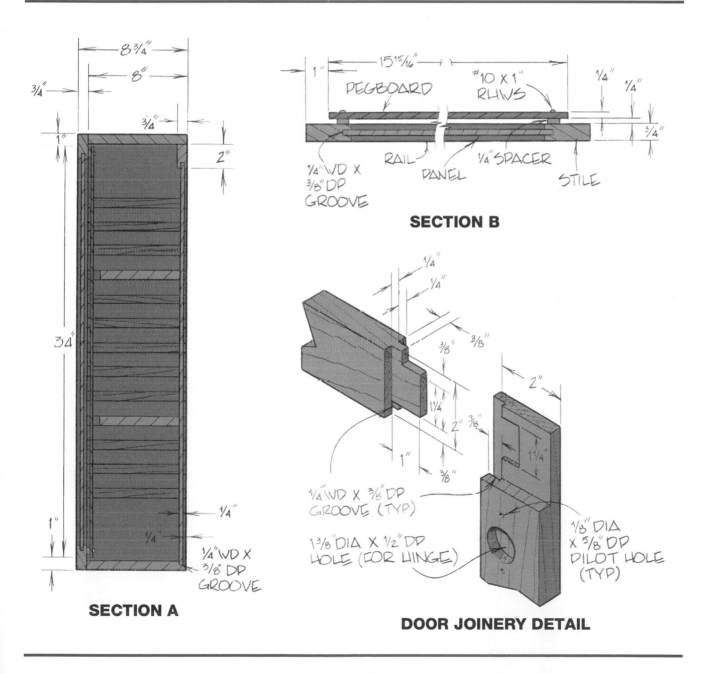

SECTION A

SECTION B

DOOR JOINERY DETAIL

3

Drill the holes needed to mount the doors on the cabinet case. European-style hinges aren't mortised into the door or the case in the normal manner; they're mounted in stopped holes. Using a Forstner bit or multispur bit, drill 1³/₈″-diameter, ¹/₂″-deep holes in the inside face of the door stiles to

hold the body of the hinge. Also, drill ¹/₈″-diameter, ⁵/₈″-deep pilot holes for the mounting screws. (See Figures 1 and 2.) The positions of these holes vary with the make of the hinge — refer to the manufacturer's directions.

1/To mount a European-style cabinet hinge, drill a 1³/₈″-diameter (35mm), ¹/₂″-deep (13mm) hole in the door stile. The position of this hole varies from one manufacturer to another.

2/Drill ¹/₈″-diameter, ⁵/₈″-deep holes for the hinge mounting screws in the stiles and the sides. The positions of these holes may also vary. Several wood-working supply companies sell templates to locate these holes, or you can make your own. Special bits are available as well.

4

Assemble the case. Assemble the top, bottom, sides, and mounting rail with glue and screws. As you assemble these parts, slide the back into position, but do *not* glue it in place. Let it float in its

grooves. Counterbore and countersink each of the screws, then cover the heads with wooden plugs. Sand the plugs and the joints clean and flush.

5

Assemble and mount the doors. Finish sand the door parts. Assemble the rails and stiles with glue, inserting the tenons in the mortises. As you assemble the doors, slide the panels in place but do *not* glue them. Let them float in their grooves. Sand all joints clean and flush, then attach door pulls to the inside stiles.

Drill ³/₁₆″-diameter holes through the centers of the spacers, and notch the outside edges of the pegboard door backs to fit around the hinges. Attach the door backs to the back surface of the doors, driving round-head wood screws with washers through the peg-board and spacers and into the door stiles, as shown in *Section B*. The panels must be centered, so their edges are 1″ from the door edges.

Mount the doors on the case with hinges, following the manufacturer's instructions. (See Figure 3.) Most of these hinges are self-closing, so you don't need a door catch on the inside of the case.

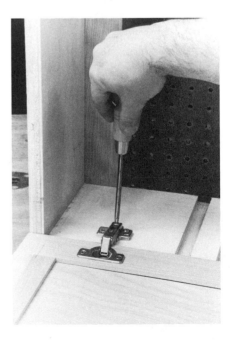

3/To install a hinge, fit the hinge body in the large hole in the door stile and secure the hinge with mounting screws. Attach the mounting plate to the inside surface of the case, then secure the hinge to the mounting plate. If needed, turn the positioning screws on the hinge to adjust the location of the door on the case.

6 **Finish the cabinet.** Remove the doors and all hardware from the case. Also remove the pegboard door backs from the doors. Apply a finish to the wooden parts. Coat all sides of the cabinet, inside and out, top and bottom. Buff the finish with wax.

7 **Hang the cabinet.** If you've built more than one cabinet and wish to hang them side by side, attach the adjoining sides with wood screws. Countersink the screws so the heads are flush with the inside surface of the sides.

Find the studs in the wall where you want to hang the cabinet. With a helper and several "deadmen" (lengths of 2 x 4, cut to support the cabinet at a predetermined height), position the cabinet (or joined cabinets) on the shop wall. Drill ¼" pilot holes through the mounting rail, then drive lag screws with flat washers through the rail and into the studs.

TRY THIS! If you're going to store anything very heavy in this project, attach a ¾"-thick, 2"-wide ledger to the wall just below the cabinets. The bottom of each case should rest on this ledger for extra support.

When you've hung the cabinet, replace the backs on the doors. Mount the doors on the case, and install the pulls.

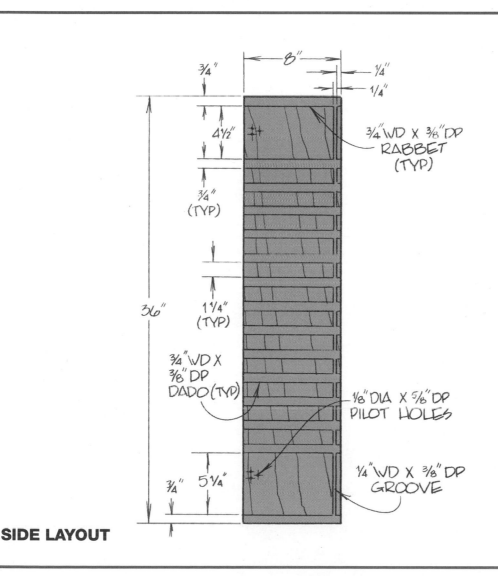

SIDE LAYOUT

8 Cut and mount the shelves.

Cut and mount the shelves. When the cabinet is up, you can better plan what you want to store and where. First, hang the tools to be stored on the pegboard. Then determine the width of the shelves by the size of the tools on the back of the doors — you don't want these tools to bang against the shelves. Cut the shelves. Finish sand them, apply a finish, and slide them in place in the cabinet.

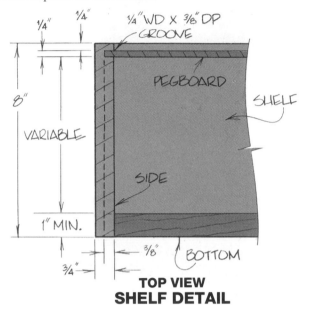

TOP VIEW
SHELF DETAIL

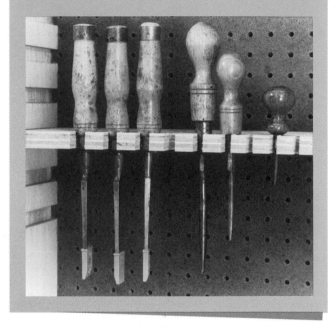

TRY THIS! You can use the shelves to hang small tools such as chisels. Drill holes, 1/2" to 1" in diameter depending on the size of the tools, through the shelves near the front edges. Then open up these holes to the front edge with a band saw or saber saw.

Using Camphor to Prevent Rust

Steel tools rust quickly in damp basements and unheated garages, even when they're properly stored in cabinets and chests. In fact, tool cabinets and chests sometimes compound the problem. These enclosures trap humid air and accelerate the rust. There is little you can do to prevent this.

You can, however, prevent moisture from harming your tools. Keep *camphor tablets* in enclosed spaces with them. These tablets are available at most drugstores and through some mail-order woodworking suppliers. The camphor slowly evaporates, then condenses on tool surfaces, coating them with a thin, oily film. This film, in turn, provides a barrier against the moisture and keeps your tools from rusting.

Keep half a tablet in small spaces (such as the drawers in the Tool Chest), a whole tablet in medium-size spaces (such as the cupboard under the Router Cabinet), and two or more tablets in large spaces (such as the Hanging Cabinet). Replace them as they evaporate and disappear.

To prevent your tools from rusting in cabinets and chests, keep camphor tablets in these enclosed spaces. The camphor slowly evaporates, coating the tools and protecting them from moisture. Replace the tablets every 2–3 months, or as they disappear.

Tool Chest

In many home work-shops, there's no good way to organize the smallest tools and accessories. The large and medium-size tools all have their place, sitting on a shelf or hanging on a pegboard. But the smallest items — nail sets, allen wrenches, needle files, and so on — usually end up in a jumble, roaming around in a drawer or box that's too big for them. What you need to organize these very small implements is a chest of very small drawers — what was once called a *machinist's tool chest*.

In the tool chest shown, there are six small drawers and a bin or "till," all less than 2½″ deep — enough small-tool storage for most home workshops. If you need more space, build the optional base for a total of nine drawers.

Or you can build several bases and stack them on top of each other to make a chest with as many drawers as you'd like. ✸

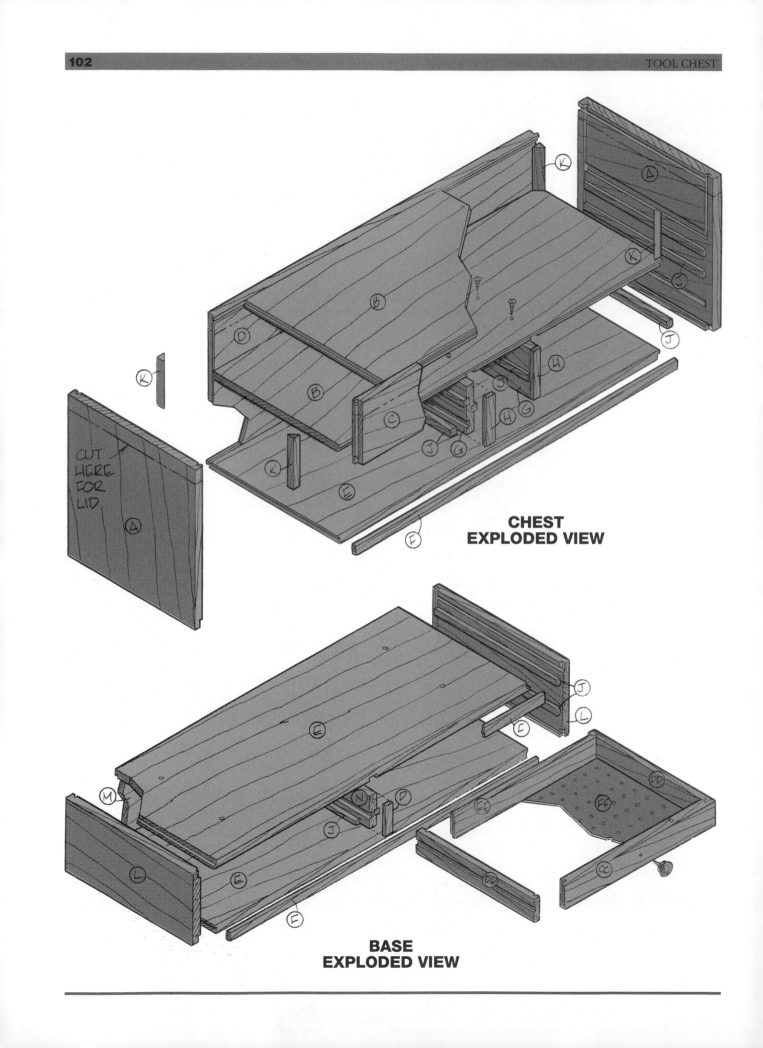

**CHEST
EXPLODED VIEW**

CUT
HERE
FOR
LID

**BASE
EXPLODED VIEW**

Materials List

FINISHED DIMENSIONS

PARTS

Chest

A. Chest sides (2) $\frac{1}{2}$" x $9\frac{5}{8}$" x $9\frac{5}{8}$"

B. Lid/till bottom (2) $\frac{1}{2}$" x $8\frac{7}{8}$" x $23\frac{1}{4}$"

C. Front $\frac{1}{2}$" x 4" x $23\frac{1}{4}$"

D. Chest back $\frac{1}{2}$" x $9\frac{3}{8}$" x $23\frac{1}{4}$"

E. Chest bottom $\frac{1}{2}$" x $9\frac{3}{8}$" x $23\frac{1}{4}$"

F. Chest bottom trim $\frac{1}{4}$" x $\frac{1}{2}$" x $23\frac{1}{4}$"

G. Chest dividers (2) $\frac{1}{2}$" x 3" x $8\frac{7}{8}$"

H. Chest divider trim (2) $\frac{1}{4}$" x $\frac{1}{2}$" x $2\frac{3}{4}$"

J. Chest drawer glides (12) $\frac{3}{8}$" x $\frac{3}{8}$" x $8\frac{7}{8}$"

K. Glue blocks (4) $\frac{1}{2}$" x $\frac{1}{2}$" x 3"

Base

E. Base bottom/top (2) $\frac{1}{2}$" x $9\frac{3}{8}$" x $23\frac{1}{4}$"

F. Base bottom/top trim (2) $\frac{1}{4}$" x $\frac{1}{2}$" x $23\frac{1}{4}$"

J. Base drawer glides (6) $\frac{3}{8}$" x $\frac{3}{8}$" x $8\frac{7}{8}$"

L. Base sides (2) $\frac{1}{2}$" x $4\frac{7}{8}$" x $9\frac{5}{8}$"

M. Base back $\frac{1}{2}$" x $4\frac{3}{8}$" x $23\frac{1}{4}$"

N. Base divider $\frac{1}{2}$" x $1\frac{3}{4}$" x $8\frac{7}{8}$"

P. Base divider trim $\frac{1}{4}$" x $\frac{1}{2}$" x $1\frac{1}{2}$"

Top Left/Right Chest Drawers* (4)

Q. Drawer fronts (4) $\frac{1}{2}$" x $1\frac{3}{8}$" x 9"

R. Drawer sides (8) $\frac{3}{8}$" x $1\frac{3}{8}$" x $8\frac{7}{8}$"

S. Drawer backs (4) $\frac{3}{8}$" x $1\frac{1}{8}$" x $8\frac{1}{2}$"

T. Drawer bottoms** (4) $\frac{1}{8}$" x $8\frac{1}{2}$" x $8\frac{3}{4}$"

Top Middle Chest Drawer*

U. Drawer front $\frac{1}{2}$" x $2\frac{3}{4}$" x 4"

V. Drawer sides (2) $\frac{3}{8}$" x $2\frac{3}{4}$" x $8\frac{7}{8}$"

W. Drawer back $\frac{3}{8}$" x $2\frac{1}{2}$" x $3\frac{1}{2}$"

X. Drawer bottom** $\frac{1}{8}$" x $3\frac{1}{2}$" x $8\frac{3}{4}$"

Bottom Chest/Base Drawers* (2)

Y. Drawer fronts (2) $\frac{1}{2}$" x $2\frac{3}{8}$" x 23"

Z. Drawer sides (4) $\frac{3}{8}$" x $2\frac{3}{8}$" x $8\frac{7}{8}$"

AA. Drawer backs (2) $\frac{3}{8}$" x $2\frac{1}{8}$" x $22\frac{1}{2}$"

BB. Drawer bottoms** (2) $\frac{1}{8}$" x $22\frac{1}{2}$" x $8\frac{3}{4}$"

Top Base Drawers* (2)

CC. Drawer fronts (2) $\frac{1}{2}$" x $1\frac{1}{2}$" x $11\frac{1}{4}$"

DD. Drawer sides (4) $\frac{3}{8}$" x $1\frac{1}{2}$" x $8\frac{7}{8}$"

EE. Drawer backs (2) $\frac{3}{8}$" x $1\frac{1}{4}$" x $10\frac{3}{4}$"

FF. Drawer bottoms** (2) $\frac{1}{8}$" x $10\frac{3}{4}$" x $8\frac{3}{4}$"

HARDWARE

1" x 23" Piano hinge and mounting screws

$\frac{1}{4}$" T-nuts (4)

$\frac{1}{4}$" x 1" Machine screws

#8 x 1" Flathead wood screws

$\frac{7}{8}$" Wire brads (10–12)

Chest latches and mounting screws (2)

Cabinet lock, escutcheon, and mounting screws

$\frac{3}{4}$" Drawer pulls (11)

$\frac{3}{16}$"-dia. x $8\frac{3}{8}$" Metal rods (2)

Metal corner protectors (8) — optional

*Cut the drawer parts to the sizes shown, then sand the assembled drawers to fit.
**Make these from pegboard.

---

1 Select the stock and cut the parts to size.

To make a chest and a single base, you need about 22 board feet of 4/4 (four-quarters) stock, and a 4' x 4' sheet of $\frac{1}{8}$" pegboard. Choose a hard, durable wood, such as maple, birch, or oak. The tool chest shown is made from curly maple.

Cut the parts to the sizes shown in the Materials List, except the chest sides, chest back, chest front, and glue blocks. Cut the glue blocks $\frac{1}{8}$" longer than specified. And add $\frac{1}{8}$" to the vertical dimension of the sides, back, and front. These alterations are to compensate for the $\frac{1}{8}$" kerf made when the lid is sawed free of the case.

Note: Precision is extremely important in this project. Use the *same* measuring tool for all of the parts. When you cut them, be sure that your saw and other equipment are properly aligned and adjusted.

2

Cut the joinery needed to assemble the chest and base. The parts of the cases fit together with simple dadoes, grooves, and rabbets. Make the 1/8"-wide joints with a table saw and a combination blade that cuts a 1/8"-wide kerf. Make the wider joints with a dado cutter or router. Several of them — particularly the stopped dadoes — must be cut with a router.

Cut the following joints, referring to the *Chest Side Layout, Base Side Layout, Chest Divider Layout, Base Divider Layout, Section A,* and *Section B:*

- 1/2"-wide, 1/4"-deep dadoes in the till bottom and base top to hold the dividers
- 1/2"-wide, 1/8"-deep stopped dadoes in the chest sides to hold the till bottom
- 3/8"-wide, 3/16"-deep stopped dadoes in the chest sides, base sides, chest dividers, and base divider to hold the drawer glides

- 1/8"-wide, 1/8"-deep stopped dadoes in the chest sides and base sides to hold the lid, chest bottom, base top, and base bottom
- 1/8"-wide, 1/8"-deep stopped grooves in the chest sides and the base sides to hold the chest back and base back
- 1/8"-wide, 1/8"-deep grooves in the chest back and chest front to hold the lid and the till bottom
- 1/8"-thick, 1/8"-long tenons in the edges and/or ends of the lid, till bottom, chest bottom, base top, and base bottom to fit the grooves and dadoes in the adjoining parts

Using a hand chisel, cut the notches in the chest sides and base sides for the trim.

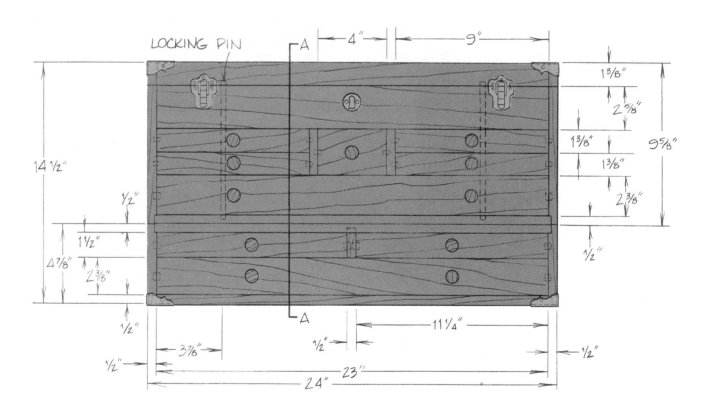

FRONT VIEW

3

Make the tongue-and-rabbet joints.
The chest and base backs are held in tongue-and-rabbet joints, as shown in the *Bottom-to-Back Joinery Detail*. These joints help absorb the blow should you knock the back of the chest or base against something. To make them, cut a ³/₈″-wide, ¹/₈″-deep rabbet along the back edges of the chest bottom, base bottom, and base top. Immediately behind each rabbet, make a ¹/₈″-wide, ¹/₄″-deep groove (measuring the depth from the surface of each board.) Then cut a ¹/₈″-thick, ¹/₈″-long tenon on the bottom edge of the chest back and both edges of the base back. These tenons will fit in the grooves.

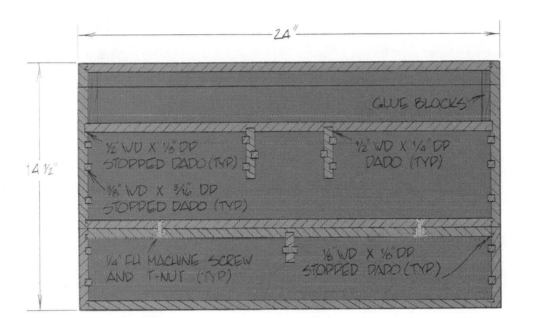

SECTION B

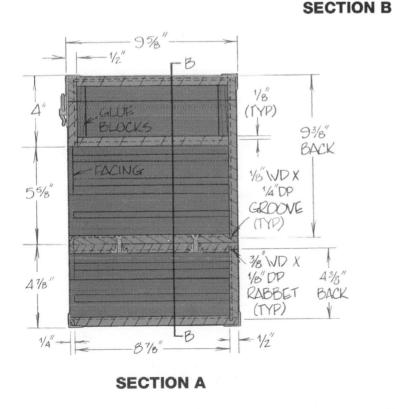

SECTION A

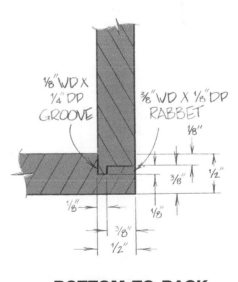

**BOTTOM-TO-BACK
JOINERY DETAIL**

4

Drill the holes needed to attach the chest to the base. The base is attached to the chest by four bolts and T-nuts, as shown in *Section B*. To be certain that the holes line up exactly, place the chest bottom on the base top and tape them together so the parts won't shift. Drill four ¼″-diameter holes through the two boards, one hole near each corner. The position of these holes is not critical, but they should be about 2″ from the corners.

Remove the tape. Countersink the holes in the chest bottom, then enlarge the holes in the base top to ⁵/₁₆″ diameter. Also, counterbore the holes in the base top to accept the bases of the T-nuts.

5

Assemble the chest and base. Finish sand the parts for the chest and base. Glue the drawer glides in their dadoes in the chest sides, base sides, chest dividers, and base divider. Let the glue dry thoroughly.

Glue the chest dividers to the till bottom and the base divider to the base top. Reinforce the glue joints with flathead wood screws, driving the screws down through the larger boards and into the dividers.

Install T-nuts in the ¼″-diameter holes in the base top. The bases of the nuts must be flush with the bottom surface of the top.

Glue together the chest sides, lid, chest front, till bottom, chest bottom, and chest back. Also glue together the base sides, base top, base bottom, and base back. Let the glue dry completely (at least 48 hours), then sand all joints clean and flush.

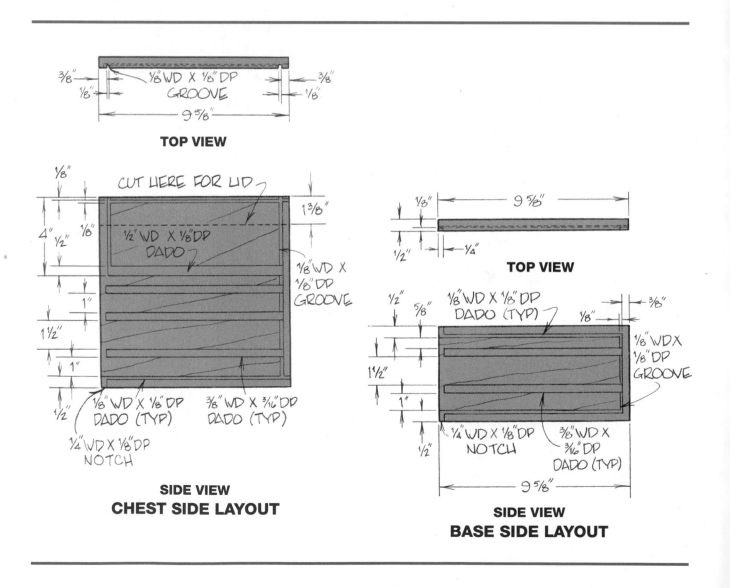

TOP VIEW

SIDE VIEW
CHEST SIDE LAYOUT

TOP VIEW

SIDE VIEW
BASE SIDE LAYOUT

6

Cut the lid free of the chest.   Use a table saw to carefully cut the lid free of the chest. Position the rip fence 1³/₈″ away from the blade, and set the blade height to ⁹/₁₆″. Placing the chest on the saw as if it were a large board, cut the front, back, and sides.

Note: Cut the front and back first, then the sides. As you make the last cut, be extremely careful not to push the chest against the fence so hard that the blade binds.

TRY THIS!   After you've cut three surfaces (front, back, and one side), put ¹/₈″-thick spacers in the kerfs and clamp the lid to the chest. Then cut the last side. The spacers will keep the lid from pinching against the chest. This, in turn, will keep the blade from binding.

7

Install the glue blocks.   Cut each glue block in two, so one part is 1³/₈″ long and the other 2⁵/₈″. Glue the blocks to the inside corners of the lid and till. The ends of the blocks must be flush with the edges of the lid and till.

8

Cut the drawer parts.   Measure the drawer openings and note any deviation from the plans. Make the necessary changes in the dimensions, then cut the parts to size. Note that the drawer parts are sized to fit the openings exactly. This will, in fact, make the drawers larger than they need to be. Sand or plane each drawer to size, custom-fitting it to its opening.

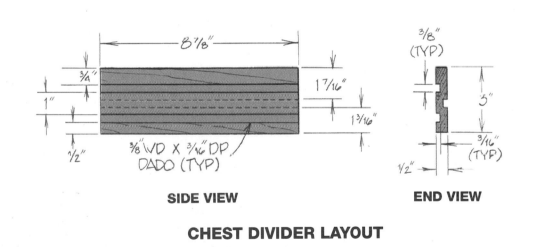

SIDE VIEW   **END VIEW**

CHEST DIVIDER LAYOUT

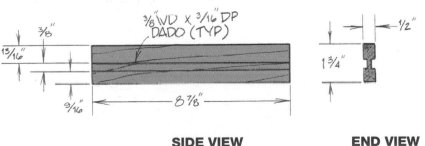

SIDE VIEW   **END VIEW**

BASE DIVIDER LAYOUT

9

Cut the drawer joinery. The sides of each drawer are joined to the front with lock joints (sometimes called dado-and-tongue joints). You can make these joints on a table saw with a dado cutter accessory, as shown in Figures 1, 2, and 3.

After making the lock joints, cut ⅛"-wide, ⅛"-deep dadoes in the sides to hold the backs, and matching ⅛"-thick, ⅛"-long tenons in the ends of the backs. Also, cut ⅛"-wide, ⅛"-deep grooves in the inside surfaces of the sides and fronts to hold the bottoms. Each groove must be ⅛" from the bottom edge.

Carefully measure the positions of the drawer glides before marking cuts for the ⁷⁄₁₆"-wide, ¼"-deep grooves in the outside surfaces of the drawer sides. Calculate the positions of these grooves from the positions of the glides. For example, if a pair of glides is ¹⁵⁄₁₆" above the chest bottom, position the grooves in the bottom chest drawer sides ¹⁵⁄₁₆" above the bottom edge.

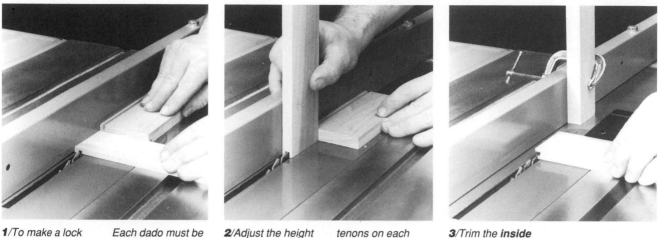

1/To make a lock joint to join the drawer parts, first cut ⅛"-wide, ⅛"-deep dadoes on the inside faces of the drawer sides.

Each dado must be ⅛" from the end of the board.

2/Adjust the height of the blade and cut a ⅛"-wide, ¼"-deep groove in the ends of the drawer ends. This will create two ¼"-long

tenons on each end.

3/Trim the **inside** tenons on the drawer ends to ⅛" long. These short tenons should fit the dadoes in the drawer sides.

10

Assemble and fit the drawers.
Assemble the drawers with glue, wiping away the excess. As you put the sides and ends together, slide the bottoms in place but do *not* glue them. Let them float in the grooves, and hold them in place by

driving a brad through each bottom into the back. After the glue dries, sand the drawer joints clean and flush. Install drawer pulls, then fit each drawer to its opening by planing, scraping, and sanding away the stock until the drawer operates smoothly.

11

Install the locking pins. Two locking pins keep the contents of the chest secure, preventing other people from opening five of the six drawers. To install these locking pins, first place all the drawers in the chest. Make sure the fronts are flush with the front of the chest.

Using a ¼"-diameter "aircraft" (long) drill bit, make two 8"-deep holes down through the top edge of the chest front, through the drawer fronts, and into the chest bottom, as shown in the *Front View*. Do not drill through the chest bottom.

Place dowel centers in the holes, then put the lid in place on the chest. Firmly press the lid down onto the dowel centers so they leave an impression. Drill a ¼"-diameter, ½"-deep hole into the edge of the lid at each mark.

Cut two ¼"-diameter metal rods 8⅜" long, and drop them into the holes in the chest. They should protrude about ⅜", so you can take them out whenever you want to open the drawers. File the burrs off the top and bottom ends of the rods.

12

Mount the lid. Mortise the lid and the chest front for a lock. Also mortise the lid and chest back for the piano hinge, then mount the lid to the chest.

When the lid swings closed, the holes in the lid front must fit over the two locking pins. Once the lid is properly mounted, install the lock, catches, and escutcheon.

13

Finish the tool chest. Remove the lid, drawers, and all hardware from the tool chest. Apply a finish to the chest, base, and drawer fronts. Coat all sides of the chest and base, inside and out, top and bottom. Apply paraffin wax to the drawer glides to help the drawers work smoothly.

Attach the chest to the base by driving machine screws down through the chest bottom and into the T-nuts in the base top. Replace the lid, drawers, and other hardware. If you wish, attach metal corner protectors. You can purchase these protectors from most mail-order woodworking suppliers.

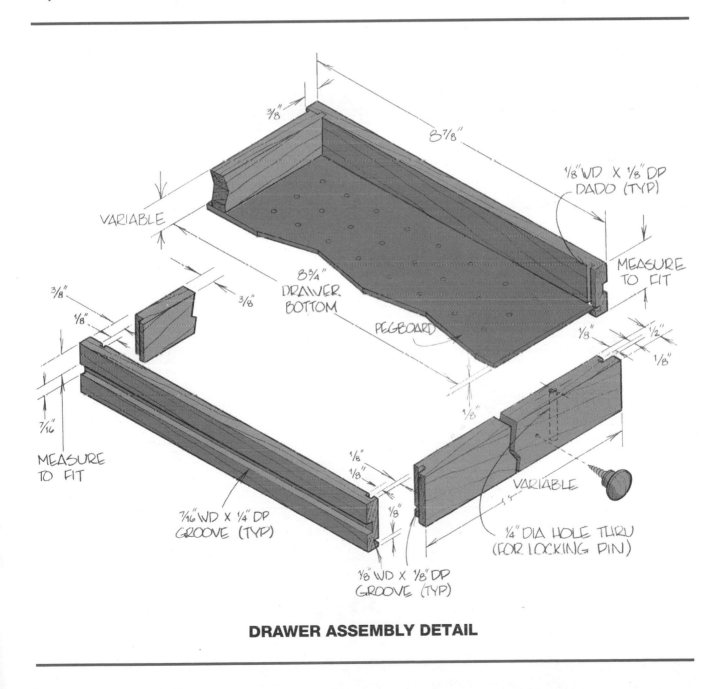

DRAWER ASSEMBLY DETAIL

Band Saw Extension Table

Most home workshop band saws have small worktables, no larger than 16″ x 16″. There is a good reason for this — a band saw is designed to make exacting cuts in small workpieces. However, every now and then you must use this tool to cut large boards. For these operations, you need an *extension table* for more support.

This plywood table fits around your present band saw worktable, extending it about 12″ in three directions. It clamps to the fence rails or, if you don't have a band saw fence, two hardwood mounting bars screwed to the worktable. The extension table has its own adjustable fence, which mounts in slots in the table. Hardwood aprons and four adjustable legs provide the additional support needed for heavy workpieces. You can attach or remove the extension table in just a few minutes.

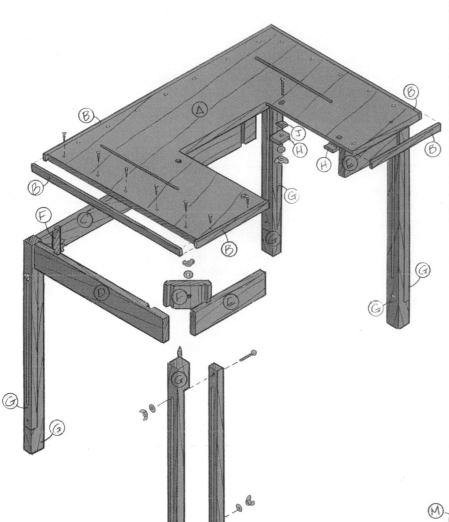

EXPLODED VIEW

Materials List

FINISHED DIMENSIONS

PARTS

A. Table* $3/4'' \times 23\frac{1}{2}'' \times 35\frac{1}{2}''$

B. Edge trim
(total) $1/4'' \times 3/4'' \times$ (variable)

C. Front apron $3/4'' \times 3\frac{1}{4}'' \times 31\frac{1}{2}''$

D. Side aprons (2) $3/4'' \times 3\frac{1}{4}'' \times 19\frac{1}{2}''$

E. Back
aprons (2) $3/4'' \times 3\frac{1}{4}'' \times$ (variable)

F. Corner
blocks (4) $3/4'' \times 3\frac{1}{4}'' \times 6\frac{1}{8}''$

G. Legs (8) $1\frac{1}{2}'' \times 1\frac{1}{2}'' \times 26''$

H. Clamps (4) $3/4'' \times 1\frac{1}{2}'' \times 3''$

J. Spacers (4)   (variable) x
$1\frac{1}{2}'' \times 1\frac{1}{2}''$

K. Fence face $3/4'' \times 3'' \times 36''$

L. Fence base $3/4'' \times 2\frac{1}{4}'' \times 36''$

M. Fence
braces (5) $3/4'' \times 2\frac{1}{4}'' \times 2\frac{1}{4}''$

*Make this from plywood or MDF board.

HARDWARE

$7/8''$ Wire brads (24–36)

#8 x $1\frac{1}{4}''$ Flathead wood screws
(36–42)

$3/8'' \times 2''$ Carriage bolts (8)

$3/8'' \times 2\frac{1}{2}''$ Carriage bolts (4)

$5/16'' \times 2''$ Carriage bolts (2)

$3/8'' \times 4''$ Stud bolts (4)

$3/8''$ Flat washers (16)

$5/16''$ Flat washers (2)

$3/8''$ Wing nuts (16)

$5/16''$ Wing nuts (2)

1

Inspect and measure the band saw table. Study your band saw and decide how you want to attach the extension table to it. If you have a fence (with fence rails) you can probably use a simple system of clamps, as shown in the *Clamp Detail*. If you don't, you may have to attach two mounting bars to the worktable, as shown in the *Alternate Mounting Detail*, then rest the table on these bars.

Carefully measure the band saw table — the thickness, length, and width. If you have a fence for your band saw, measure the fence rails and how far they sit below the surface of the worktable. Also measure how long and how wide the rails are. You'll need these measurements to determine other dimensions as you build the extension table.

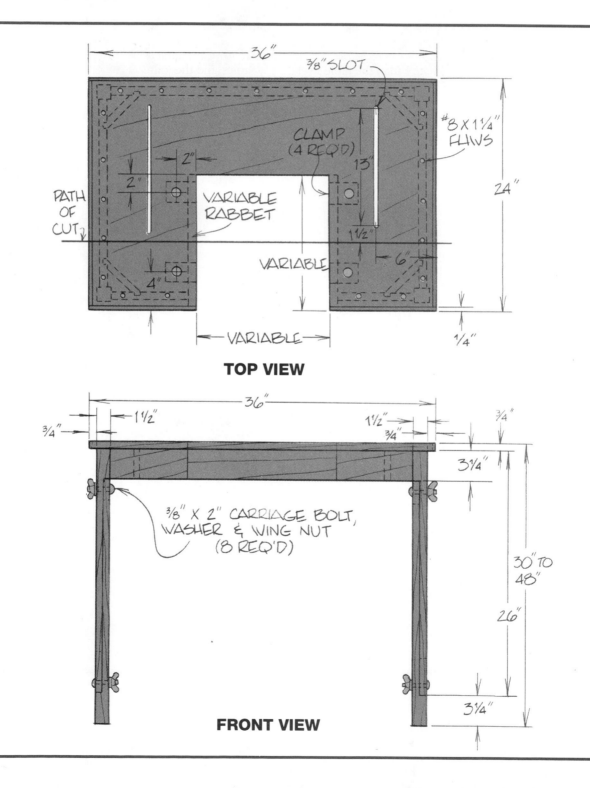

TOP VIEW

FRONT VIEW

2

Select the stock and cut the parts to size. To build this project you need about 4 board feet of 4/4 (four-quarters) stock, 8 board feet of 8/4 (eight-quarters) stock, and a 2′ x 4′ sheet of ¾″ plywood or MDF board. Select a very hard wood such as maple, birch, or oak — these wear better than softer woods. When you have selected the stock, cut the parts to the sizes specified in the Materials List, except the table trim. Don't cut the trim to length until after you've made the table.

3

Cut and trim the table. Lay out the cutout for the band saw worktable on the table, making it about ⅟₁₆″–⅛″ deeper and wider than the table itself. Cut out the waste with a saber saw. Cut the trim to fit the table, and attach the trim to the edges with glue and brads. Sand the joints clean and flush.

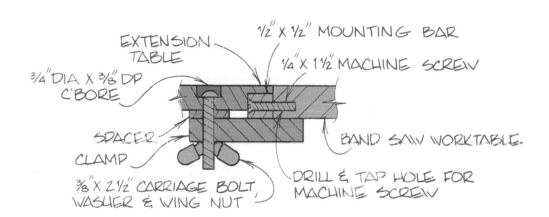

ALTERNATE MOUNTING DETAIL

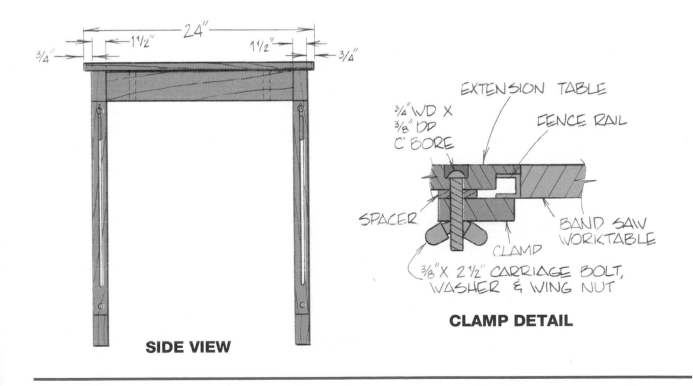

SIDE VIEW

CLAMP DETAIL

4

Cut the necessary joinery. Using a table saw, dado cutter, or router, cut the joinery needed to assemble the table. First, cut ³/₄″-wide, ³/₈″-deep dadoes in the ends of the aprons to hold the corner blocks, as shown in the *Leg-to-Apron Assembly Detail*. Then cut away half the stock for 22³/₄″ of the length of each leg as shown in the *Leg Layout/Side View*.

Using a router, cut rabbets in the underside of the table on both sides of the worktable cutout. These rabbets should be slightly wider than the fence rails or mounting bars. Calculate the depth of the rabbets by subtracting the distance that the rails or bars sit below the worktable from ³/₄″ (the thickness of the extension table).

Note: Make the rabbets ³/₈″ deep if you are using the alternate mounting system. Later, attach the mounting bars ³/₈″ below the worktable surface (³/₄″ minus ³/₈″ equals ³/₈″).

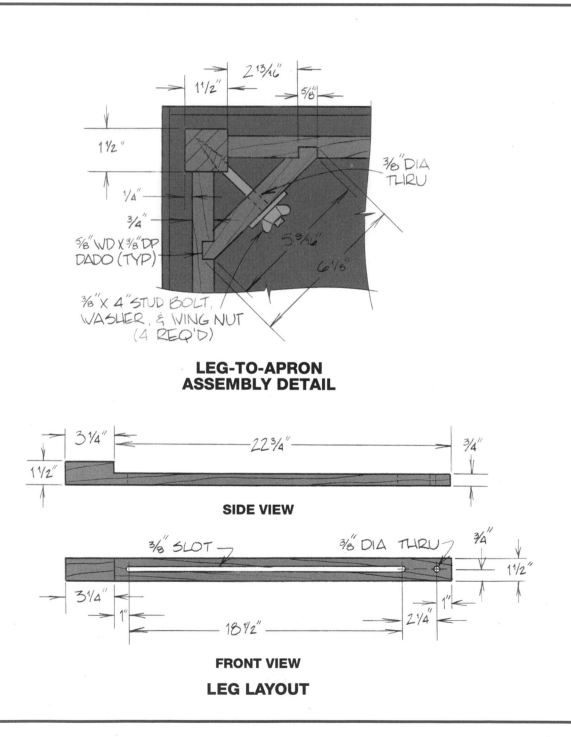

LEG-TO-APRON ASSEMBLY DETAIL

SIDE VIEW

FRONT VIEW

LEG LAYOUT

5

Drill the holes needed. Drill the holes needed to assemble and attach the extension table:

- ³/₄"-diameter, ³/₈"-deep counterbores in the top side of the extension table for the bolts that attach the table to the band saw, as shown in the *Clamp Detail* or the *Alternate Mounting Detail*
- ³/₈"-diameter holes through the table counterbores
- ³/₈"-diameter holes through the spacers
- ³/₈"-diameter holes through the clamps
- ³/₈"-diameter holes through the legs for the adjusting bolts, as shown in the *Leg Layout/Front View*

- ³/₈"-diameter holes through the center of the corner blocks, as shown in the *Leg-to-Apron Assembly Detail*
- ⁵/₁₆"-diameter holes through the fence base, as shown in the *Fence/Top View*

If you're using the alternate mounting system, drill two ¹/₄"-diameter holes through each mounting bar. (The positions of these holes depend on where you want to attach the bars to your band saw worktable.) Countersink the holes for machine screws.

Note: Make the mounting bars from a very hard wood.

6

Make the corner blocks. The legs are held to the aprons by stud bolts and corner blocks. These blocks allow you to easily remove the legs from the table when you want to store it.

To cut the tenons on the blocks, saw four bevel cuts across the ends of the blocks, all at 45°. (See Figure 1.) Adjust the table saw blade to 45°, and position the rip fence for use as a guide. Start cutting by making one side of a V-groove near the ends of all four blocks. Make a pass, then flip the blocks end for end and make another. Readjust the position of the fence and

cut the other sides of the grooves in all the blocks. (See Figure 2.)

After you've cut the grooves, cut a narrow bevel and a wide bevel across each end. (See Figures 3 and 4.) Once again, use the rip fence as a guide, and flip the blocks to make identical cuts in each end.

Note: The rip fence must be positioned very accurately for the last two cuts. If the fence is too close to the blade on either cut, you'll shorten the block on the second-to-last pass. The last pass will be off, making the block asymmetrical.

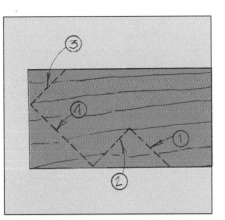

1/To make the corner blocks, saw four bevel cuts in each end of each block. Make the cuts in the order shown, and use the rip fence to guide your work.

2/First, make two cuts at 45° to form V-grooves near the ends of the blocks.

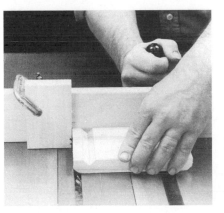

3/After cutting the V-grooves, make the narrow bevel cuts on the ends of the blocks.

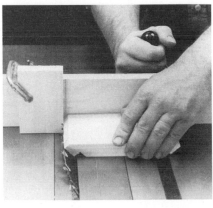

4/Finish the blocks by cutting the wide bevels. The rip fence must be positioned very accurately when you make these last miter cuts. You want a double miter on the end of each block, but you don't want to shorten the blocks when you make the last miters.

7 Rout the slots in the table and legs.

Both the legs and the fence are adjustable. The legs are bolted to each other, and the fence to the extension table. The bolts all slide in slots so you can position the components where you need them. Using a router and a ³/₈″-straight bit, cut 13″-long slots in the table and 18¹/₂″ long slots in the legs, as shown in the *Top View* and *Leg Layout/Front View*. (See Figure 5.)

5/To rout a slot in a leg, first clamp the leg between two 2 x 4s, as shown. This will help support the base of the router while you work. Nail a strip of scrap wood to one of the 2 x 4s to guide the router.

8 Assemble the table.

Finish sand all parts. Glue the spacers to the clamps. The hole in each spacer must line up with the hole in the clamp. Sand the glue joints clean and flush.

Turn the table upside down. Lay out the aprons and corner blocks on the underside of the table. Mark the position of the parts, then drill ¹/₈″-diameter pilot holes through the table. Countersink these holes on the top side of the table.

Glue the corner blocks and aprons together, inserting the ends of the blocks into the dadoes in the aprons. Before the glue dries, attach the aprons and blocks to the table with glue and flathead wood screws.

Drill ⁵/₁₆″-diameter pilot holes in the inside corners of the top legs. Mount the legs in V-blocks to hold them at the proper angle to the bit as you drill. Install the stud bolts in the legs — put a hex nut on the stud-end of each bolt, then turn the lag-end into its pilot hole with a wrench. Remove the hex nut. Insert the stud bolts through the holes in the corner blocks. Put flat washers and wing nuts on each bolt and hand tighten.

Insert bolts in the ³/₈″-diameter holes in both the top and bottom legs. As you slide a pair of legs together, insert the bolt of each leg into the slot of the other. Again, put flat washers and wing nuts on each bolt and hand tighten.

9 Attach the table to the band saw.

If you are using the alternate mounting system, remove the worktable from your band saw. Mark the positions of the mounting bars on the worktable. The top surface of each bar must be ³/₈″ below the top surface of the worktable. Drill holes through the edges of the table and tap these holes for ¹/₄″-20 threads. Attach the mounting bars to the table with machine bolts, then replace the worktable on the band saw.

Slide the table in place around the band saw worktable. When the rabbets are resting on the fence rails or mounting bars, the extension table surface should be flush with the worktable. Insert carriage bolts in the holes in the table. Put the clamps, flat washers, and wing nuts over the bolts. Turn the clamps so they overlap the fence rails or mounting bars, and hand tighten the nuts. Adjust the length of the legs so they support all four corners of the table.

10 **Assemble and attach the fence.** Miter one corner of each fence brace at 45°, as shown in the *Fence/Side View.* Then assemble the fence face, base, and braces with glue and flathead wood screws. Countersink the screws so the heads are slightly below the surface of the wood.

Place the fence on the extension table, centering the holes in the fence base over the table slots. Insert carriage bolts down through the base and the table. Put washers and wing nuts on the bolts and tighten them so they're snug, but not tight.

> **TRY THIS!** To be sure that a fence is perfectly straight and square, joint the face and the base *after* you assemble the fence. Make certain that the screw heads are well below the surface of the wood before you do this.

11 **Finish the extension table and fence.** Remove the fence from the extension table, the extension table from the band saw, and the legs from the extension table. Remove all the carriage bolts, washers, and wing nuts from the table, legs, and fence.

Do any necessary touch-up sanding, then apply a finish to all wooden surfaces. Wax the top surface of the table to help the work slide across it smoothly. Then reassemble the table, legs, fence, and hardware.

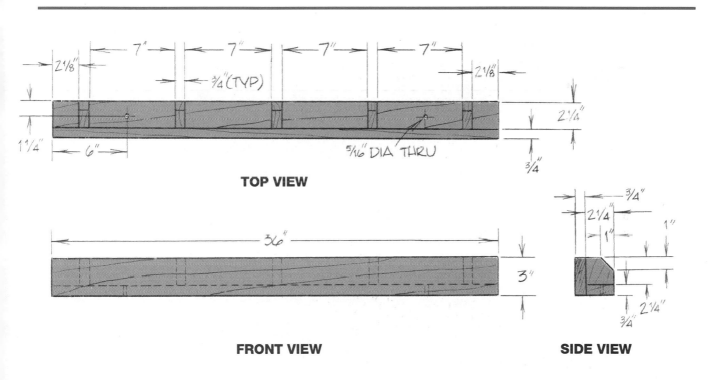

TOP VIEW

FRONT VIEW   **SIDE VIEW**

FENCE

Storage Shed Wood Rack

Do you need to store a large amount of lumber, keep woods sorted by type and size, or stack green lumber to dry? If so, this simple rack will help you do all of these things simply and inexpensively.

This is actually more than a simple rack; it's an entire lumber storage *system* with several different components. The wall-mounted and center-mounted *lumber racks* store ordinary boards. They are designed so you can place boards in the racks from either the side or the end — this makes it simpler to retrieve any one board. The *plywood bin* stores large and small sheet materials on edge — not just plywood but also particleboard, pegboard, and so on. The *overhead racks* store sheet materials that must rest flat, such as drywall and certain hardboards. You can pick and choose the components of this system that you need or have room for.

Build the lumber rack components from ordinary construction-grade 2 x 4s and 2 x 2s, and install them in any commercial or home-built storage shed. The shed shown is larger than most, but this rack can be adapted to almost any size. You can also install it on just one side of a shed, and use the remaining floor space to store other materials. ✸

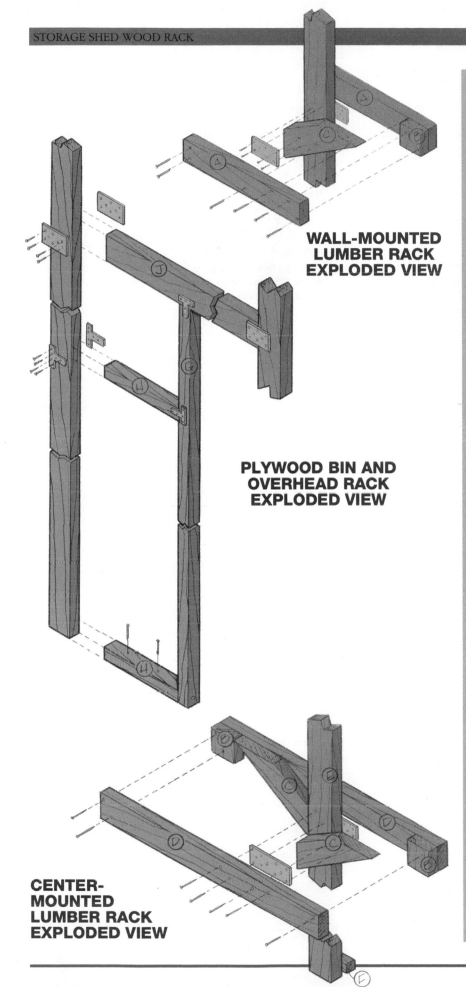

WALL-MOUNTED LUMBER RACK EXPLODED VIEW

PLYWOOD BIN AND OVERHEAD RACK EXPLODED VIEW

CENTER-MOUNTED LUMBER RACK EXPLODED VIEW

Materials List

FINISHED DIMENSIONS

PARTS

Wall-Mounted Lumber Racks (5)

A. Short arms (10)   1½″ x 3½″ x 19½″
B. Spacers (5)   1½″ x 3½″ x 3½″
C. Braces (5)   1½″ x 3½″ x 14⅜″

Center-Mounted Lumber Racks (5)

B. Spacers (10)   1½″ x 3½″ x 3½″
C. Braces (10)   1½″ x 3½″ x 14⅜″
D. Long arms (10)   1½″ x 3½″ x 35½″
E. Wide posts (5)   1½″ x 3½″ x (variable)
F. Cleats (5)   1½″ x 1½″ x 3½″

Plywood Bin

G. Narrow posts (5)   1½″ x 1½″ x (variable)
H. Rails (10)   1½″ x 1½″ x 12″

Overhead Racks* (5)

J. Crossbeams (5)   1½″ x 3½″ x (variable)

*As designed, the overhead racks will safely support one ton (2000 lbs.), the equivalent of 28 sheets of ¾″ plywood or 34 sheets of ½″ drywall. If you need to store more than this, make the cross-beams from 2 x 6s rather than 2 x 4s.

HARDWARE

Wall-Mounted Lumber Racks (5)

16d Common nails (60)
1½″ Roofing nails (60)
Metal gussets (10)

Center-Mounted Lumber Racks (5)

16d Common nails (100)
10d Common nails (20)
1½″ Roofing nails (120)
Metal gussets (20)

Plywood Bin

10d Common nails (60)
T-shaped gussets (30)
1½″ Roofing nails (180)

Overhead Racks

16d Common nails (0–10)
1½″ Roofing nails (60–240)
Metal gussets (10–40)

1 Plan the wood rack.

Plan the wood rack. Measure the interior width, length, and height of your storage shed. Also determine how much room you need to store the other items in your shed — lawn mower, garden tools, etc. Then decide how many of the lumber rack components you have space for. Should you install wall-mounted lumber racks, center-mounted racks, or both? How many do you have room for vertically and horizontally? Do you have room for a plywood bin? Overhead racks? Do you have enough room left over to get sheet materials in and out of the bins and racks easily? Here are some points to consider:

- Any one component requires at least five racks, spaced 24″ on center, to support an 8′-long board.
- Walkways between the racks or bins should be at least 18″ wide.

- The plywood bin shouldn't be too wide — no more than 12″ between the wall and the posts. If you need more plywood storage, add additional posts and longer rails.
- Overhead racks should be at least 50″ wide to accommodate 4′-wide sheet materials.
- If the plywood bin or overhead racks are against one side wall, there should be at least 4′ of clear space *in front* of them to maneuver sheet materials in and out of the shed door. If not, place the bin and racks so they're centered in front of the door.

Sketch a simple front view of the wood rack you have in mind on a piece of graph paper, similar to the *Sample Wood Rack Plan* shown. Indicate how the components are tied together.

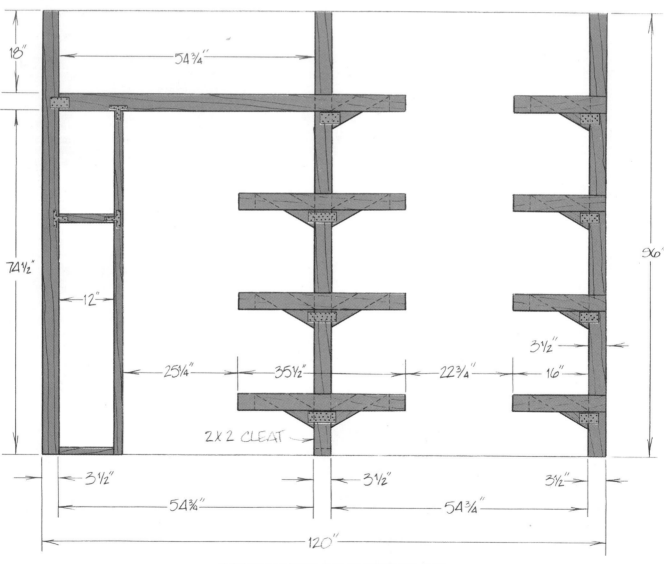

SAMPLE WOOD RACK PLAN

2

Cut the parts to size. When purchasing the materials, specify #2 lumber — this is slightly stronger than ordinary construction grade. The amount of materials you need will depend on the number of components you install in the shed. Use your plan to figure out how much lumber you need, then purchase it. Cut the parts to the required sizes. Miter the ends of the braces at 60° and 30°, as shown in the *Brace Layout*.

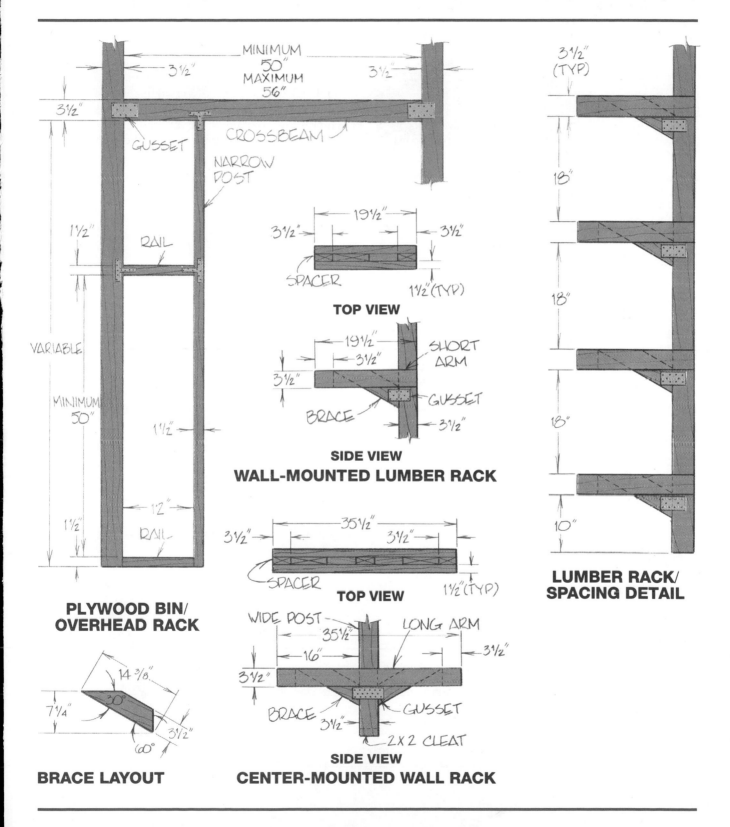

PLYWOOD BIN/ OVERHEAD RACK

WALL-MOUNTED LUMBER RACK

TOP VIEW

SIDE VIEW

LUMBER RACK/ SPACING DETAIL

BRACE LAYOUT

TOP VIEW

SIDE VIEW

CENTER-MOUNTED WALL RACK

3

Assemble the lumber racks. Wall-mounted or center-mounted lumber racks, if your plan includes them, are easier to assemble *before* you install them in the shed.

For wall-mounted racks, lay out the arms, spacers, and braces on a flat surface. (Use a 2 x 4 scrap to space the arms apart where they will fit against the studs in

the shed wall.) Nail the parts together with 16d nails, but don't nail them to the scrap. (See Figure 1.)

For the center-mounted variety, first check that the posts fit properly in the shed, but do *not* nail them in place. Again, lay out the arms, spacers, braces, and posts on a flat surface. Assemble them with 16d nails, roofing nails, and metal gussets. (See Figure 2.)

1/Preassemble the arms, braces, and spacers for the wall-mounted wood racks. Then all you have to do to install them in your shed is nail the arms and braces to the studs.

2/Also preassemble the center-mounted racks, attaching the arms, braces, and spacers to the posts. Then you can install the post (with the racks attached) in your shed.

4

Install the racks and bins in the shed. Using a level, plumb bob, and snap line, measure and mark the positions of all the components in the shed. Attach the components to the shed frame and floor with 16d nails, roofing nails, cleats, and metal gussets.

Wall-mounted wood racks — Attach the arms to the studs with 16d nails, and the braces to the studs with gussets and roofing nails.

Center-mounted wood racks — Attach the top ends of the posts to the rafters, joists, or crossbeams with 16d nails. Nail 2 x 2 cleats to the floor with 10d nails, then attach the bottom ends to the cleats.

Plywood bin — Attach the top ends of the narrow posts to the joists, rafters, or crossbeams with metal gussets and roofing nails. Attach the bottom rail to the floor with 10d nails, then nail the bottom end of the post to it. Attach the top rail to the wall studs and post with gussets and roofing nails.

Overhead racks — Attach the crossbeams to the wall studs or posts, using 16d nails or gussets and roofing nails — whichever works best. Attach the upper ends of the braces to the rails with gussets and roofing nails, and the lower ends to the studs or posts with 16d nails or gussets and roofing nails. Once again, use whichever fastener works best.

Note: You don't have to brace the end of a crossbeam if it's supported by a post, as shown in the *Sample Wood Rack Plan.*

TRY THIS! When nailing a part to an unsupported post or rail, back up the stock with a *nailing anvil.* This is a small, dense piece of iron that fits comfortably in the palm of your hand. Start the nail in a board, then hold the anvil against the opposite side of the board while you drive the nail home. The mass of the anvil will keep the unsupported stock from bending with each hammer blow.

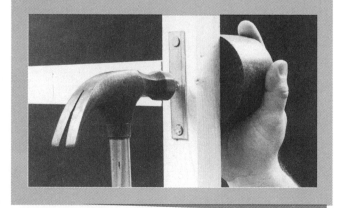

Note: If the floor of your shed is concrete, attach the rails and cleats to it with expansion shields. Drill holes in the floor with a masonry bit, insert the shields in the holes, then secure the wooden parts with lag screws.

Credits

About the Author: Nick Engler is a contributing editor to *American Woodworker* magazine, and teaches cabinetmaking at the University of Cincinnati. This is his nineteenth book on woodworking.

Contributing Craftsmen and Craftswomen:

Larry Callahan (Sandpaper Dispenser, Clamp Racks)

Judy Ditmer (Work Cart, Knockdown Assembly Table, Clamp Racks)

Nick Engler (Plywood Cutting Tables, Dust Control Cart, Work Island, Quick Cabinets, Router Mortising Jig, Double-Support Sawhorses, Table Saw Cutoff Box, Hanging Cabinets, Storage Shed Wood Rack)

Hugh Garvin (Router Cabinet)

Jim McCann (Tool Chest)

Virgil Schmidt (Clamping Aids, Band Saw Extension Table)

Special Thanks To:
    Heartwood, Tipp City, Ohio
    Lifestyle Woodworking, Vandalia, Ohio
    Wertz Hardware Store, West Milton, Ohio

Rodale Press, Inc., publishes AMERICAN WOODWORKER™, the magazine for the serious woodworking hobbyist. For information on how to order your subscription, write to AMERICAN WOODWORKER™, Emmaus, PA 18098.

WOODWORKING GLOSSARY

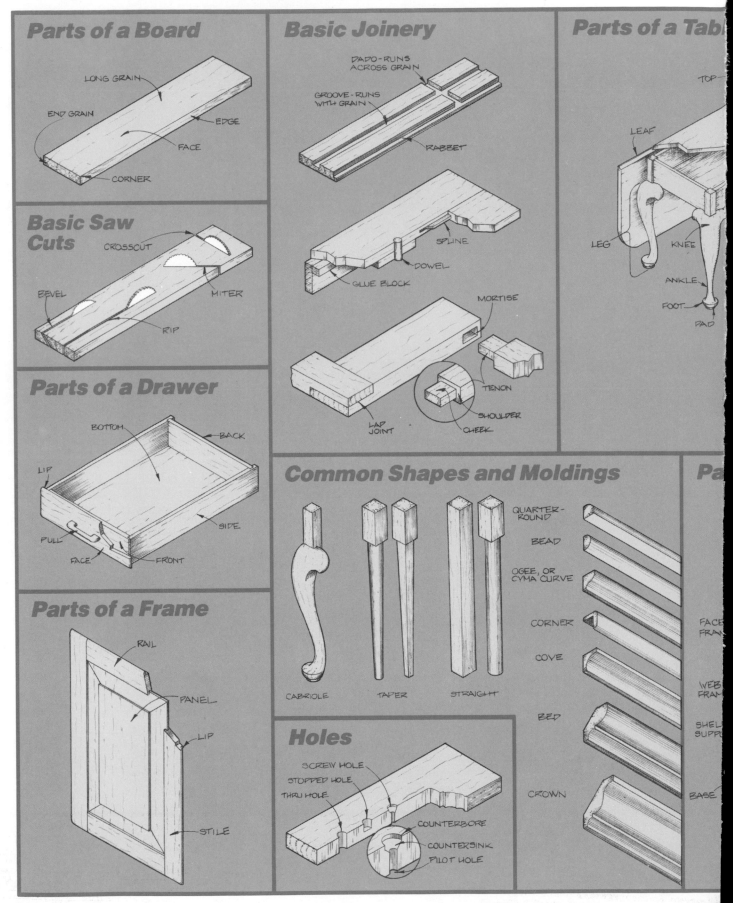

Parts of a Board

LONG GRAIN
END GRAIN
EDGE
FACE
CORNER

Basic Saw Cuts

CROSSCUT
BEVEL
MITER
RIP

Parts of a Drawer

BOTTOM
BACK
LIP
SIDE
PULL
FACE
FRONT

Parts of a Frame

RAIL
PANEL
LIP
STILE

Basic Joinery

DADO - RUNS ACROSS GRAIN
GROOVE - RUNS WITH GRAIN
RABBET
SPLINE
DOWEL
GLUE BLOCK
MORTISE
TENON
SHOULDER
CHEEK
LAP JOINT

Parts of a Tab[le]

TOP
LEAF
LEG
KNEE
ANKLE
FOOT
PAD

Common Shapes and Moldings

CABRIOLE
TAPER
STRAIGHT

QUARTER-ROUND
BEAD
OGEE, OR CYMA CURVE
CORNER
COVE
BED
CROWN

Holes

SCREW HOLE
STOPPED HOLE
THRU HOLE
COUNTERBORE
COUNTERSINK
PILOT HOLE

Pa[...]

FACE FRA[ME]
WEB FRAM[E]
SHEL[F] SUPP[ORT]
BASE